FEB 2016

P9-CFK-168

DISCARD

D0166263

I,

SPY

I,

SPY

HOW TO BE
YOUR OWN
PRIVATE
INVESTIGATOR

DANIEL RIBACOFF

St. Martin's Press
New York

DISCLAIMER: This book is for informational purposes only. Some of the methods and techniques discussed in this book may be governed by federal, state or local laws and regulations, and certain activities may raise the interest of law enforcement professionals.

Nothing in this book should be interpreted as legal advice. Neither the publisher nor the author is engaged in rendering legal services. Before engaging in the activities discussed in this book, readers should seek the services of a competent legal professional.

Note to Readers: The names and identifying characteristics of a few individuals depicted in this book have been changed.

I, SPY. Copyright © 2016 by Daniel Ribacoff. All Rights Reserved. Printed in the United States of America. For information, address St. Martin's Press, 175 Fifth Avenue, New York, NY 10010

The Library of Congress Cataloging-in-Publication Data is available upon request.

ISBN   978-1-250-07135-4 (hardcover)
ISBN   978-1-4668-9253-8 (e-book)

Our books may be purchased in bulk for promotional, educational, or business use. Please contact your local bookseller or the Macmillan Corporate and Premium Sales Department at 800-221-7945, extension 5442, or by e-mail at MacmillanSpecialMarkets@macmillan.com.

First Edition: February 2016

10 9 8 7 6 5 4 3 2 1

R0444748050

CONTENTS

INTRODUCTION

CHAPTER 1: Eye on the Street: Physical Surveillance — **1**

CHAPTER 2: Eye in the Sky: Electronic Surveillance — **23**

CHAPTER 3: Go Get 'Em: How to Find Anyone Anywhere — **37**

CHAPTER 4: True Crime: How to Tell if Someone Is Lying — **55**

CHAPTER 5: Proof Positive: How to Gather Evidence — **79**

CHAPTER 6: Out of Site: How to Virtually Disappear — **105**

CHAPTER 7: Safe House: How to Protect Your Home, Business & Valuables — **117**

CHAPTER 8: Identity Theft: How to Protect Your Privacy — **139**

CHAPTER 9: Back Off, Pal: How to Protect Yourself — **155**

CHAPTER 10: Private Eye, Public Eye: How to Protect Your Fellow Man — **179**

CHAPTER 11: What Would Dan Do? — **195**

ACKNOWLEDGMENTS — **203**
RESOURCES — **204**
FURTHER READING — **213**
INDEX — **214**

INTRODUCTION

Everybody wants to know the truth.

Your next-door neighbor says your kid hit a baseball through his front window, but your son says the guy's nuts. Who's telling the truth? Your husband has been coming home late for the past two weeks and complains he's been slammed with work. Do you believe him? Or do you suspect that he's cheating on you? A young man applies for a job at your firm, and you don't know him from Adam, but his resume's stellar and he looks like a good kid. Should you hire him? Has he been fired from other jobs? Is he setting you up for harassment or for a hostile work environment lawsuit? How can you find out?

Private investigation is about digging through layers of lies and deception and coming out on the other side with that kernel of truth, the fact behind the fiction—and the evidence to prove it. It's about finding and filtering information, getting what's coming to you, and protecting what's important to you. It's about getting to the bottom of a situation using your noodle and your know-how. And, with a little training and practice, you can do it like a pro.

WHO AM I?

For many years, my family owned a Midtown Manhattan diamond company and jewelry manufacturer, founded in 1979 by my father, a retired engineer. You want to know about theft and security and having eyes in the back of your head? Try being a diamond dealer. One day, my father went into the office early in the morning in order to meet with a courier from a jewelry store in a neighboring county. The doorbell rang, and my father answered the door to see that the courier had brought another man with him—both were armed with guns, a lead pipe, and an ice pick.

When security arrived within minutes, my father was unconscious on the floor. Portions of his scalp were hanging off from having been beaten with the lead pipe, and his shirt was bloody from being stabbed with the ice pick. My father survived the attack, but

SITUATIONS
IN WHICH YOU MIGHT EMPLOY INVESTIGATIVE TECHNIQUES

- To obtain evidence of infidelity
- To locate someone, be it a loved one, a birth mother, or someone who owes you money
- To conduct a background check on a person—a potential spouse, son-in-law, business partner, or employee
- To locate assets
- To go off-grid

is legally blind to this day. The courier's accomplice was caught and served twenty-five years in prison. The courier, however, managed to escape. They never found him.

Around this time, I joined the New York City Auxiliary Police, a team of volunteers who assist their local police precincts, housing police service areas, and transit districts. I served as a sergeant in the citywide special task force and received numerous awards of merit and commendations, including one from the National Police Hall of Fame. We performed uniformed patrol and were recruited, trained, and equipped by the New York Police Department (NYPD). (I served the NYPD until 1994 and have been serving the Nassau County Police Department as an auxiliary cop since 2006.) We did street patrol in every precinct in the city and worked special events—Jets games, parades, you name it. We were there for Mayor Ed Koch's first inauguration. I learned everything there was to know about New York City as an auxiliary cop—the people, the streets. Neighborhoods that you never even thought of going to, we went to. And there was no GPS back then. In those days, if you didn't know where you were going, you didn't know where you were going, so you really learned your way in and around the city fast.

In 1990, I started the International Investigative Group. I came up with the idea of offering consulting investigative work for people like my father and others who worked jobs in industries that dealt in valuables and for which security was of utmost importance. I began working with Lloyd's of London, Tiffany & Co.'s insurance company, and other firms that insured jewelers, jewelry stores, traveling jewelry salesmen, and jewelry manufacturers.

For two years, I was a diamond dealer by day and private eye by night. I just put a phone on the wall and answered it every time it rang—at the time, I had two kids, and my wife was pregnant with our third—until I could get the private investigation business up and running. I would come home at night, type reports, do research (remember, there was no Internet back then) until four o'clock in the morning, get up a few hours later, and go back to work in the jewelry business.

Slowly, through word of mouth, the business grew. My first private investigative job was for Harry Winston; I investigated a courier who claimed he was robbed of $750,000. I branched out from there—armored truck losses, million-dollar burglaries, worker's comp investigations, auto accidents, domestic suits. I put up my sail and went wherever the wind took me, building my investigative business one brick at a time.

Within a few years, I began studying with an established polygraph examiner—a real old-timer, with forty years' experience under his belt. He was a little guy with a Hitler mustache, a bad toupee, and a deep voice, but when you spoke to him on the phone, you'd think he was six foot nine. He started throwing me some investigative work so he could focus on polygraphing, more commonly known as *lie detecting*. He became my mentor, and years later, after he passed away, I incorporated polygraph services into my own business. I also studied formally under one of polygraph and forensic interviewing's foremost researchers, Nathan J. Gordon, the director of the Academy for Scientific Investigative Training in Philadelphia, Pennsylvania, as well as William L. Fleischer, who serves as assistant director of the academy and is a former FBI and U.S. Customs polygraph expert.

THE STEVE WILKOS SHOW

The business grew steadily over the years, and I started getting calls to do TV—I did technical consulting for the *Guiding Light* soap opera, where I set up a polygraph scene for an actor playing a detective, and I appeared on the National Geographic Channel as well as programs such as *The Tyra Banks Show, The Millionaire Matchmaker, Impractical Jokers*, and the *Today* show, among many others.

In early 2009, I got a call from *The Steve Wilkos Show*, a syndicated daytime talk show hosted by Steve Wilkos, who once served as director of security for *The Jerry Springer Show*. The producers were looking to hire a polygraph examiner in the New York tri-state area—at the time, NBC was moving production for shows such as *Jerry Springer, The Steve Wilkos Show, Maury*, and *Deal or No Deal* from Chicago to Connecticut. I was like, *Deal or No Deal*? I get to see the models? I love Model 21! I went for the interview, they liked me, and I began working for them that year.

A former Chicago cop, Steve Wilkos is a great guy and a great interviewer. We sort of make a Lone Ranger and Tonto type of team. Since I've been there, the show has focused more on criminal investigation rather than relationship topics. We cover everything from murder to molestation. I'm their polygraph guy. They turn to me to help weed out the liars—guy comes on, says he never cheated on his girlfriend, and then, after conducting a thorough polygraph exam, I deliver the report to Steve that says whether the guy's telling the truth or is full of crap.

Most times, even before I conduct a formal polygraph test, I can tell if someone's lying. The signs of deception are there, and I'm always surprised that more people can't recognize them. It's a good skill to have. Virtually everyone has something to gain from learning the fundamentals of lie detection and other basic investigative skills. They're applicable to business owners, parents, spouses, school administrators, and more. Want to keep tabs on your kids? Your employees? Want to track down that old flame of yours from high school? Want to know if your wife is running

DID YOU KNOW?

In 1833, Eugène François Vidocq, a French soldier and convict turned crime fighter, founded the first private detective agency known as Le Bureau des Renseignements Universels pour le commerce et l'Industrie (The Office of Universal Information for Commerce and Industry). Vidocq is said to have taken the investigative profession out of the French underworld, elevating it to a social science and inspiring the work of authors such as Sir Arthur Conan Doyle and Victor Hugo, among others. Today, the Vidocq Society is a members-only crime-solving club that meets every month in Philadelphia; members try to crack unsolved crimes, particularly murder.

around on you? Want to pull a *Home Alone* on a would-be burglar? You can.

During my years as an investigator, many people have contacted me with requests for very simple jobs that they can do themselves. They just don't realize it. A lot of investigation is common sense. And, nowadays, there is so much information available online that makes detective work, particularly background checks or locating assets or people, so much easier. Most of the research I conduct is through public records—the key is knowing where to find information, how to access it, and how to interpret it.

WOULD YOU MAKE A GOOD PRIVATE INVESTIGATOR?

Basic investigation is pretty easy, but it's important to note that nearly all fifty states require private investigators to be licensed, and many government municipalities are cracking down on unlicensed operations. This means that you, as a civilian, cannot open a business as an unlicensed private eye, nor can you conduct investigations for hire. The purpose of this book is to help you perform your own private investigations—for personal matters—with strategies used by the pros in order to keep you and your loved ones safe. That said, virtually anybody, with lots of practice, can learn to do this type of work, but there are certain qualities that a successful investigator will likely have.

1. Are you willing to work around the clock?
There are no set hours when it comes to private investigation. It's not Monday through Friday, nine to five. Many times, you're working during holidays, weekends, snowstorms, whatever it might be. Sometimes you'll be on a surveillance job and "sit on" a guy for sixteen, seventeen, eighteen hours straight. You've got to be willing to put in the time.

2. Are you willing to do your homework?
For licensed professionals, private investigation is a para-law enforcement–type of position. You often have to testify in court, so you have to be sure you're familiar with the legal dos and don'ts. Amateur sleuths also need to be familiar with lawful matters, such as citizens' rights and privacy laws. You don't want to do anything illegal or get sued civilly.

3. Do you have a good poker face?
Sometimes you have to lie to find the truth. Police officers and private investigators do it all the time. Once, I was conducting a surveillance, and a guy comes up and knocks on my car window:

"What are you doing here?" he asked.

"I'm an auto repossessor," I said without hesitation.

"Whose car are you here to repossess?"

"I can't tell you that, because then the guy's not going to give me the car."

"You're not here to repossess my car, are you?"

"Do you have a Mercedes?"

"No."

"Then you're okay, bro."

And he left me alone. As long as you look and act credible—and you're polite, respectful, and not breaking the law—you're likely to be believed.

GLOSSARY

Sit on: Conduct a stakeout or stationary surveillance.

Tail: Conduct a moving surveillance.

4. Can you act?

Sometimes lying isn't enough. And if you're trying to gather information by subterfuge, you've got to be able to play different roles. Today, I'm a news reporter working on a big story. Tomorrow, I'm your old high school classmate looking to organize a thirty-year reunion. Or I'm doing a background check for an employer. Or I'm your long-lost Uncle Pete. (Trust me, when it comes to acting, Meryl Streep's got nothing on me.) Can you convince somebody that you're someone else? As a private eye, you may have to.

5. Are you willing to travel out of your neighborhood?

A friend of mine is a veterinarian. He owns a chain of clinics and, at this point in his career, just does the management, so he's bored. He comes to me and says, "I'd love to be a private investigator. It seems so exciting. Would you hire me?" I said, "Yeah. I need you to interview a couple of people in the Marcy Houses project in Brooklyn." He goes, "Are you kidding? I'm not going to the housing project." Guess what? Then you can't be an investigator. Everybody thinks it's glamorous all the time. Trust me, it's not. We often rate neighborhoods by how many guns we need to carry to work there—a one-gun, two-gun, or three-gun neighborhood. We go to some really bad places. If you're a private investigator, you can't say, "I'm going to work here, but I'm not going to go there." You've got to go where the job takes you.

6. Are you willing to travel out of your comfort zone?

Remember the Motorola beepers? Everybody had a beeper in the nineties. We used to have a beeper that had a little pinhole camera with a wire that you could attach to a video recorder. My guys would put it in a knapsack and walk the streets of Manhattan like a messenger, and they'd have the beeper in their pocket and could film people in public areas. One time, an insurance company executive said to me, "This girl was in a car accident. She says she can't work. We think she's working. I need proof." She was an exotic dancer in New Jersey. We followed her, and she went to this place called Heartbreakers, a strip club. I put one of my best agents on the case, a Puerto Rican guy named Carlos. (You can put a Latino guy anywhere—in the city, in the suburbs, on a farm—and he'll fit in.)

I said, "Carlos, you have to get footage of this girl working, dancing. Be careful, because they search you when you go into these clubs, and you can't get caught with a camera." So Carlos goes into his car, breaks down the camera equipment, sticks it in his crotch, knowing they won't search him there, and when he gets inside the place, he goes into the bathroom and puts the camera back together. Then he sticks the unit back in his pants and puts the beeper cam right through his shirt, puncturing a hole for the wire.

He takes a seat near the stage. All the dancers come out and get into a circle, and here comes the girl who's supposed to be injured dancing up a storm. She's not wearing a back brace, obviously, because she isn't wearing much. Guys all along the bar are giving her ten bucks, and she's pulling open her bikini top and letting them have a squeeze. So Carlos turns on his camera, and what do I see? The girl comes dancing over to Carlos, and he gives her ten dollars. She opens her top, and he starts squeezing her boob. I'm like, "Carlos, we have to show this in court to the judge, and here's my insurance investigator squeezing the stripper's boobs." Carlos says, "I had to do it. Everybody else was doing it. If I didn't, I wouldn't blend in." He was right! This is the kind of craziness you wind up doing as an investigator.

7. Can you be adaptable?

GLOSSARY

Target:
The person (also called a subject), object, or place under investigation or being watched.

Expect the unexpected when it comes to private investigation. I had a client who wanted me to follow her husband. No problem. She says he's planning a trip to the Poconos in Pennsylvania to go fishing with his friends. I put two agents on him. The guy has a Ford Expedition, and my agents have little Hondas. They could barely keep up with him. Suddenly, the husband starts driving north, instead of west, toward New England. He keeps going and going and going. My guys call me up and say, "We're in Vermont, and we're running on fumes." I said, "Don't stop." I mean,

P.I. GLOSSARY

Conflict of interest: A situation where a person has a duty to more than one person or organization.

Once, a client told me he thought his wife, who was a nurse, was messing around with a male coworker, another nurse. "They get off work at seven A.M., and I want you to follow her," he told me. So I followed them as they left work in the wife's minivan. They wound up driving to a Long Island railroad station to have sex. I couldn't believe it. They're having sex as commuters are going to work! I recorded the whole thing, she was totally busted, and that was that. I got a call about a month later from the wife's attorney, whom I happened to know. He told me he had a female client who needed work done on her husband, Tony, who owned a Carvel ice cream store and worked for the sanitation department. It was the same couple! I asked, "Is his wife's name Suzy?" He said yes. I said, "I can't. It's a conflict of interest." He said, "You did that video? Man, that was a good video." It's a small world.

what can you do? If you stop for gas, you're never going to find him again. Finally, when they're practically sputtering, the guy pulls into a motel and meets his girlfriend. Here we thought he was going to the Poconos, and he ends up in Vermont. You just never know. Once you get onto that highway, you could be gone for one day or six.

8. Can you be discreet?

One of my part-time guys, Bill, previously was an FBI surveillance operative. He's a real nebbishy, nerdy guy—no girlfriend, no wife. Whenever I had a city surveillance, I'd use him as a foot agent. I'd go with Bill and a couple of other agents on a job to follow a target, and I'd say into my phone, "Bill, the target is looking in the window at Men's Wearhouse." And Bill said, "Yeah, I've got him." Meanwhile, I'm looking around and thinking, *Where the hell is Bill?* You can't even see him. Bill's disappeared. That's how good he is. As a private investigator, you have to be like a chameleon and blend. If people are staring at you, you're not doing your job.

9. Do you have a network of friends to help you out?
Private investigators will often utilize teams of operatives—the more sets of eyes and ears, the better. When I have a surveillance in the city, I'll use two agents—at the very minimum—to watch all the various exits and entrances of a subject's building, essentially creating a ring around him. It can be tough. I've had jobs where five or six agents still weren't enough, and we wound up losing the target. It pays to have friends!

10. Are you tech savvy?
So much of private investigation is done on the computer these days—locating assets, tracking people—that you need to have basic skills, such as how to use search engines and social media, or how to operate a digital camera or voice recorder.

11. Have you got chutzpah?
To do investigative work, you have to have guts, chutzpah, cojones. You have to be willing to put yourself into risky or potentially dangerous situations. Remember, you're usually dealing with lowlifes, liars, and bottom-feeders—dads who skipped out on their families, mothers who stole from their children, employees who schemed their bosses. You've got to track them down, interact with them, and come off cool as a cucumber even if you're shaking in your boots.

One time, I was working with the NYPD on an insurance investigation and wearing a wire in order to enter the home of a very high-ranking member of the Gambino crime family. I was posing as a buyer who was on the lookout for stolen artwork. I needed to collect evidence for intent. The cops were waiting outside, so if I got into trouble, I was supposed to say a code word—in this case, "How 'bout those Mets?"—and the police would come barreling in. Turns out, the operation went smoothly, but it could have just as easily gone the other way. Of course, different jobs call for different skill sets. Conducting an online search from home in your footie pajamas won't involve too much physical risk.

12. Can you think on your feet?

I used to do a lot of disability and Workers' comp investigations for insurance companies when I first started out. We often performed what is called a telephone activity check, where I would try to develop a pattern of when a target was home and when he wasn't home so I could plan a surveillance.

Now, how can I call someone constantly and not raise his suspicion? By creating a pretext of some kind. Sometimes I would say I was calling from the programming department of a television station for the purposes of conducting a survey to see what TV shows the subject was watching. I would tell people that if they cooperated with me, I would send them a gift certificate—and I would actually send them one. (Otherwise, I would be defrauding them.)

Sometimes I would call a subject up and pretend to be one of those annoying religious fanatics. I would say, "This is Virgil. I'm calling to praise the Lord." Most people would hang up, and then I would call back again and say something like "How come you have so much hatred in your heart for the Lord?" and they would usually hang up again, but I would start to get a feel for when they were and weren't home. Even though I kept pestering them, most people didn't think anything of it. They'd hate me, but they wouldn't be suspicious.

One time, however, things didn't go quite as planned.

"Is Richard home?" I asked when a woman picked up the phone.

"Yes, who's calling?" she said.

I said, "This is Virgil. I'm calling to praise the Lord."

She said, "Oh, hallelujah, brother. I go to church every day, and my husband is reading the Bible now."

I was stunned. I said, "May I read you some passages from the scripture?"

"Yes!" she said.

Meanwhile, I don't have a Bible in front of me. My secretary at the time, Jean, was a religious woman, and she was whispering,

"Bible.com . . . Bible.com." So I go on Bible.com and start reading a passage. That lady almost busted me!

Sometimes, I'll bypass the phone and go directly to people's front doors. I'll have an agent pose as a handyman and have him wear some tools, a tool belt, and a clipboard—the whole shebang—to find out if a subject is at home. He'll knock on the door and say, "I'm here to fix the dishwasher." The person will usually open the door and say, "I didn't call anybody to fix the dishwasher." My agent will pretend to be befuddled and ask, "Isn't this 321 Smith Street?" Meanwhile, he knows Smith Street is the next block over. The person will most likely say, "No. That's the house behind me." Then the agent apologizes, tells the person to have a nice day, and he's achieved his mission.

One time, Nelson, one of my agents, was on assignment in New Jersey. I needed him to ID a claimant, so he strapped on his tools and knocked on the guy's door:

"Hi, I'm here to fix the dishwasher," he said.

"Great!" the guy said. "I've been waiting for you all morning!"

What?! Nelson's pulse quickened, but he went inside and followed the guy into the kitchen. Nelson opened the dishwasher door, stuck his head inside the unit, and said, "What's wrong?" Meanwhile, he had no clue what he was doing. . . .

"It's not heating," the guy said.

Nelson scribbled something down on his clipboard. "I'll have to call this in and come back," he said. "You need a part."

Then he ran out, called me up, and told me this story. I was *dying!* (I asked him what the guy looked like. He said, "Just like Captain Crunch." What did I report to my client? *The claimant looks exactly like Captain Crunch.*) Now that's what I call thinking on your feet!

Even if you haven't answered yes to these questions, do you have a willingness to learn? Are you tired of being ripped off? Scammed? Treated like a victim? Are you a curious or suspicious person by nature? Once, a client told me that he was concerned about the guy living with his ex-wife. "I don't know much about him," he said, "but the guy is creepy, and he's doing homework with my kids." While I was on the phone with him, I ran a background check on the guy's license plate, and he turned out to be a wanted sexual predator from Florida—there was a warrant out for his arrest! I said, "Hang up and call the police!" The cops ended up pulling the guy out of the ex-wife's house in handcuffs!

Nowadays, it's important to arm yourself with the knowledge and the tools you need to: 1) seek out the truth, and 2) keep you and your loved ones safe. Therefore, I've divided this book into two sections: *how to get the bad guys* and *how to keep the bad guys from getting you*. As a private investigator, I deal with both investigation and security, and I want to teach you the strategies pertaining to each of these fields. In the first half of the book, you'll learn how to conduct a surveillance, both physical and electronic; how to locate people, evidence, and assets; and how to identify whether someone is telling you the truth. In the second half, you'll learn how to lay low or even disappear (for now or for good); how to protect your home, your business, and your valuables; how to protect your identity and your data; how to protect yourself physically; and, finally, how to protect your fellow man.

You really have to be prepared for everything—and you can be. With tried-and-true methods and tips learned on the gritty streets of New York City, this book will show you how. ▪

EYE
ON THE STREET:
PHYSICAL
SURVEILLANCE

All of us have seen movies where the grizzled gumshoe trails the bad guy down a dark alley into a secret door or where a pair of police detectives sits in an unmarked car, ribbing each other and eating fast food during a stakeout. Looks cool, right? Exciting? Fun?

The truth is: **Surveillance is tough work**. There's a lot to know and a lot to do. Real-life gumshoes and police detectives train very hard for many years to do the job right. You've got to be able to blend—to see as much as possible without being noticed yourself. You've got to be able to track someone and monitor his or her behaviors for hours, or sometimes weeks, and log or process the information gathered. You've got to, on occasion, go without food or sleep or both, all in the name of getting your man. Or woman. It's a tall order, and one not to be taken lightly.

RISKS OF PHYSICAL SURVEILLANCE

Although there's nothing illegal about conducting a physical surveillance, there are possible risks of breaking the law:

- **Traffic violations:** You need to obey the traffic laws to the best of your ability. Careless or reckless driving will not only get you in trouble, but can cause harm to others. You don't want to hit a kid. If you have an accident because of a negligent act, you will be held liable.

- **Assault or physical injury:** You can't be knocking down old ladies while you're chasing a guy.

- **Trespassing:** Entering private property without the consent of the landowner in order to obtain a photo or video violates trespassing laws. Plus, whatever information you gather will be inadmissible in a court of law.

- **Roping and entrapment:** You often hear about these issues on television shows, such as *Law & Order*. Roping, or pretexting, is obtaining information by means of legal deception. Entrapment is creating a condition in which the target of an investigation is required to perform a certain action. In other words, if you're on a disability assignment, and want to prove a guy is perfectly healthy even though he's collecting disability checks, you can't drop a handkerchief on the floor in order to video him bending over to pick it up. You can't let the air out of his tires, so that you can take photos of him jacking up his car. Your role as investigator is to be a bystander. You need to let the guy screw up on his own.

- **Stalking and harassment:** Stalking is defined as instilling fear into a person; harassment as aggressive pressure and intimidation. If you're following someone, and she discovers you and asks, "Why are you following me? Why are you harassing me?" The jig is up. You have to leave. Whether you

ARE YOU BREAKING THE LAW?

- You're following around an employee whom you believe is stealing money from you. She catches you, says she feels threatened, and warns you to stay away from her or else she'll call the cops. You think she's bluffing, so you continue to shadow her. **You've just committed a crime!** (Depending upon the type of stalking or harassment, the offense can either be a misdemeanor or a felony.)
- Your ex-husband has had you served with an order of protection, because he says you've been following him around and saying he has a girlfriend. You tell him where he can shove his order and keep tailing him. **You've just committed a felony!** You ask your girlfriend, Cathy, to follow him around instead, because the order of protection is against you, not her. Guess what? Now, *she's committed a felony*, because she's operating under your direction.

are a licensed private investigator or a private citizen, you have to go away. Of course, you can try again in a few days—wear a disguise, change cars, change your technique, try to find some other place to watch from. But if she sees you and complains about it, or files a complaint, then you are essentially stalking her and can be arrested.

- **Order of protection:** Sometimes there are orders of protection involved. An order of protection is issued by the court to limit the behavior of someone who harms or threatens to harm another person. If a target has had an order of protection issued against you, you cannot conduct a surveillance of that person. We get a lot of obsessed boyfriends, girlfriends, husbands, and wives all the time who want to hire us for surveillance, but we have to tell them we can't do it if there's an order of protection. We'll get arrested. And so will they.

PRE-SURVEILLANCE

Before you conduct a surveillance, you first want to get to know the area in which you'll be working. This is called pre-surveillance. Drive by the neighborhood during your lunch hour. Visit a few of the stores, if it's a mall or a shopping center. Get to know the parking signs on the street.

It's always best to physically visit a location, so you can get a good feel for the place, but if that's not possible you can also look at maps or, with today's technology, visit the area virtually by consulting Google Earth, Google Maps, or similar services. These tools allow you to obtain a tremendous amount of detail, so you don't have to creep around like you do during an on-site visit. You can establish good vantage points, see what vehicles are parked in driveways (fortunately, Google Maps provides you with a month and year for when its images were taken, so you can determine if the information is current), locate possible exits, and identify traffic flow. Also, Google Maps can provide you with information regarding live traffic situations, such as construction zones and road closures.

What kinds of details should you be looking for? Let's say you're watching the girl with whom you think your husband is having an extramarital affair. Your theory is, *I'll watch her instead of watching him, because she doesn't know who I am.* Good. What kinds of details would you need to know?

P.I. GLOSSARY

Felony: a higher-level crime, usually punishable by more than one year in prison.
Misdemeanor: a lower-level crime, usually punishable by less than one year in prison.

- What trains are near her house?
- What bus lines run there?
- Does she have a car?
- Are there any one-way streets?
- Is there an underground garage in her building?
- What highways are nearby? Can she jump on one or get to a road where all of a sudden traffic is very fast?
- If you drive to the surveillance area, and she starts walking to the train, can you ditch your car in a legal parking spot? Are there any around?

- Do you need a parking sticker to park in a town or city lot? If so, where can you buy one?
- Do you need a MetroCard? An E-ZPass?

P.I. GLOSSARY

Intel: Short for intelligence.

These are the kinds of questions you need to ask in order to prepare. However, even with the best preparation, things don't always go according to plan. For instance, you might begin to follow her—say, you've already gotten your parking sticker—but she nabs the last spot in the lot, and you miss the train. Or you get stuck behind a bus. It happens. But what have you learned? That she leaves the house at 7:45 A.M. That she drives to the train station and doesn't walk. Now, you can anticipate that scenario next time, and maybe have a friend hold a parking spot for you, so that when you follow her the next day, you can call your friend and say, "Susie, she's here." Your friend pulls out, you pull in, and—voila!—you have a parking spot.

A lot of times, on the first day of a surveillance, you take it from zero to one, and then you have to come back the next day and take it from one to two. Just like the military. Make a plan, but, depending on circumstances, be prepared to alter that plan. If an army unit goes to infiltrate a location with five soldiers, but when they get there, they go, *Holy crap, there are three hundred guys here!* They pull back and make a new plan. Don't be so rushed to execute everything in one day. If you see there's an obstacle, learn what you've learned today, and pick it up tomorrow. Haste makes waste. Think smart. Gather intel.

STATIONARY (OR FIXED) SURVEILLANCE

Stationary surveillance, also known as a stakeout, is being the proverbial fly on the wall. It's when an investigator stays in one place—indoors or out— to observe a target. Investigators use stationary surveillance all the time and for any number of reasons. Usually, we want to see if a person is doing what he is supposed to be doing—or doing what he's not

P.I. GLOSSARY

Burned: When an investigator has been exposed— the target has become aware that he is being watched. *If I hadn't walked so close to him, I wouldn't have gotten burned.*

supposed to be doing. *My ex-husband is not paying child support, and he says he's not working, but a friend of mine told me they saw him working at Luigi's Pizzeria.* You'll want to plan a stationary surveillance and get some evidence. I had a target once who worked as a salesman for a medical equipment company, and somebody told his boss, *Hey, do you know this guy is also selling water bottles while he's selling medical equipment?* Sure enough, we did a fixed surveillance, and, lo and behold, while the guy's on the clock for his boss, he's quenching thirsts everywhere!

Also, we'll run a stationary surveillance when an individual has a non-compete clause in his contract and chooses to ignore it, which is illegal. In other words, if you work for me as a private investigator and you get fired or you leave, you're not supposed to work for another private investigator in Nassau County, New York. The clause is in the contract I have my employees sign. If, while conducting a stationary surveillance, I find you working for another private investigator, I can now sue you for breach of contract.

Fixed surveillance is a different story every day, and every day poses a different challenge. Today, I can park in front of your house and watch you. Tomorrow, there's a road crew there, and I can't. Or they've closed off the road, there's an accident . . . Everything is fluid. There's no rubber-stamping like at the DMV. Not in this business.

STAKEOUT ESSENTIALS

In order to have a successful stakeout, you want to think like an investigator. What will you need? You want to have everything on hand, because you can't be running to the grocery store in the middle of a job—you can potentially lose your target or get burned. Here is what my guys bring along when they run a fixed surveillance:

- **Pee bottle (wide-mouth bottles for the ladies).** Any FBI agent will tell you that this is Number One in surveillance. Hands down.

- **Water.** You need to stay hydrated (remember, the more water, the more pee bottles). Go to Costco and stock up.

- **Snacks.** Keep in mind you don't know how long you'll be there, so bring lots of goodies—stuff that you like and that doesn't have a shelf life. Leave the meat and produce at home.

- **A friend.** If you're going to be out for an extended period of time, having a friend with you will let you alternate duties—one can sleep, one can watch. If you're a woman, maybe for safety reasons—depending upon the target—you might want to have a friend with you as well.

- **Binoculars.** Most compact binoculars usually offer 7x to 10x magnification ranges and are easy to store or strap around your neck. For the larger magnifications, such as 12x to 16x, you might need to bring a tripod to stabilize the binoculars. (Note: Night goggles are optional for rural areas with no streetlights; however, they are pricey.)

- **Cell phone.** Obviously, this can be used for communication, but it can also be used as a camera.

Inside of a Surveillance Van

QUICK TIP

When packing for a surveillance, instead of folding your clothing, which is how you would normally fill a suitcase, do what they do on submarines: roll your clothing. You'll be able to fit a lot more, and your clothes won't wrinkle.

• **Digital camera.** Although most cell phones offer cameras with comparable zooms, some investigators prefer stand-alone digital cameras for stills or video.

• **Adaptor.** To charge electronics in the car. Don't leave home without it!

• **Flashlight.** For reading at night. Or you can download a flashlight app to your smartphone.

• **Dark or inconspicuous clothing.** When choosing your clothing, you want to wear something that's not going to make you stick out. Usually, a pair of jeans and a black shirt will suffice, but it depends on where you are. If you're going to watch a church, you want to look like you're a churchgoer. If you're going to downtown Manhattan on a weekday, you don't want to wear cargo shorts and a T-shirt—you want to wear business attire. If you're going to a baseball game, you want to try to look like you're a person going to a baseball game, so you'll wear a sports jersey and cap.

• **A change of clothes.** During a surveillance, you often need to be a chameleon and change your appearance at a moment's notice. So wear a blue baseball cap, and carry a red one. Keep elastic bands on your wrists so you can put your hair up in a quick ponytail. Replace your regular glasses with prescription sunglasses. Wear a reversible jacket or a black shirt over a white T-shirt, so you can remove the black shirt if you need to. Start walking with a limp using a collapsible cane you just took out of your backpack. It takes a person three times to really recognize someone—three times, unless you're easily identifiable with tattoos or piercings that are memorable. Make it so even if your target has spotted you on several occasions, as far as he's concerned, he only saw you once. And, remember, if he already knows you, it will only take one time before he recognizes you.

**QUICK TIP** If you're conducting a stationary surveillance from your car in the dead of winter, be sure to run the engine periodically to clear out the windows and to get yourself some heat (same goes for the summer and air-conditioning). Don't run the engine all the time, because this will only draw attention to you—the white smoke coming out of your tailpipe will make you stick out like a sore thumb and will also waste gas. And remember to crack your windows a little bit to prevent any carbon monoxide buildup.

- **Seasonal and/or appropriate dress.** When choosing clothing, pay attention to the weather. You don't want to get hypothermia, so if it's cold, dress in layers as if you're going skiing. Use hand warmers and foot warmers. If it's 105 degrees out, face it: you're just going to sweat. The fact is, if you're in North Dakota and there's a snowstorm, you've got problems. If you're in Florida and it's 120 degrees in the car, you've got problems. Surveillance is a brutal investigative art, because no matter where you are, you're exposed to the elements.

- **Full-windshield sunshade.** If you're monitoring a target from a vehicle, a sunshade can offer additional concealment, preventing people from seeing you through the front window.

- **Vehicle paperwork.** Your car should be inspected and your registration current, just in case the traffic cops are out and patrolling the area.

- **Identification (i.e., driver's license).** There's nothing illegal about conducting a stakeout, but if the police roll up on you, they may cite you for *This is a no-parking zone* or *You've been parked here for more than an hour, and it's only an hour parking.* One time, we did surveillance in Old Westbury, New York, and there was no parking allowed on any street. The cops came around and said, "There's no parking." I'm like, *Dude, really?*

FOUR BELIEVABLE STAKEOUT COVER STORIES

1. "I'm waiting for my son. I think he's cutting school."
2. "My car broke down, and I'm waiting for a ride." (Make sure you've pulled a spark plug or something out of your engine.)
3. "Officer, I have three little kids at home. I just need a little time to myself. You understand." (Have a book on your person or in the car.)
4. "I'm waiting for my wife. She works in this office building."

Come on, you have nothing better to do? Still, you have to make sure that you're operating within the vehicle and traffic laws. Things need to be proper.

- **A believable cover story.** Again, there's nothing illegal about being on a stakeout, but you don't necessarily have to tell the cops what you're doing, because you run the risk of ruffling a few feathers or even blowing your cover. Let's say you're watching the smoothie store across the street, because you want to prove that your husband, who is not paying you child support, is working there, and it turns out that the place is full of law enforcement officers—the cops go there for smoothies all day long. If a cop decides to ask what you're doing, and you say, "I'm watching my husband who's working in the smoothie store," then, I'm telling you now, the cop will give you right up. *You know your wife's sitting outside watching you.* You want to have a cover story that's something like: *My son is supposed to be in school, and I understand that he goes to this store every day. I want to catch him cutting.* It has to sound feasible. It has to sound plausible. Lots of times, if we're doing a matrimonial case, we'll tell the police we're doing an insurance case. If I'm watching somebody for disability, I'll tell them I'm doing a matrimonial. We want to steer observers away from what's going on in order to maintain our cover.

CAN I REALLY LIE TO A POLICE OFFICER?

Lying to a police officer, in and of itself, is not unlawful, as long as you're not otherwise breaking the law (you don't have anything illegal on your person or in your vehicle, etc.). You don't necessarily have to tell the officer that you're conducting a surveillance, because there are no loitering laws, generally speaking. They don't really exist anymore. You have the right to hang around. It's a free country, as they say. Therefore, if you're legally parked on Main Street in Small Town, USA, then you're not committing a crime. (However, keep in mind that parking in a mall or hotel parking lot may be considered trespassing, because it's private property.)

What if the cops tell you to move along anyway? You don't necessarily have to. You can say, "I'm not breaking any law. I'm sitting here waiting for my son. I'm legally parked. My vehicle is registered. I'm not intoxicated. I have nothing illegal. I'm not leaving. I know my rights." Sometimes you have to be a little belligerent. If they continue to insist, you can tell them to call their sergeant or that you're going to video-record the interaction. Trust me, nobody wants to get jammed up and wind up as the lead story on *CBS Evening News*.

Another thing to keep in mind: If a police officer asks, "Can I search you?" And you say, "Yes," and he searches your person and finds marijuana . . .well, you consented to the search. If he had no probable cause, and he asks, "Can I search you?" Your answer can be no. *What's your probable cause to search me?* "Do you want to empty your pockets onto the hood?" *No.* A lot of times, people agree, because they get scared or they think they have to comply. You have to know your rights. Again, it's very important that you're not trespassing, that you're not violating the law, that your vehicle is registered, and that you can present your ID. If all that is copacetic, you don't have to leave and you don't have to tell the police exactly what you're doing. However, always be polite and respectful.

KEYS TO AN EFFECTIVE STATIONARY SURVEILLANCE

Okay, so you've got all your equipment and proper paperwork, now let's talk logistics. Even though there are many variables that

BEST CARS FOR A STAKEOUT

- A car that won't be recognized. If the target—an ex-wife, an employee—knows your vehicle, and you can't get that much distance between you, you may have to rent a Zipcar, because if you just stand on the sidewalk, you're going to stick out.
- A car with colors that blend into the environment. Dark gray or black works well in the city, whereas dark green or brown is more appropriate for rural areas. Stay away from white, red, and bright colors.
- An average-looking car, like the Honda Accord or Honda Civic. A Hummer is not good.
- A car with tinted windows. This keeps the target—as well as passersby—from being able to see you and adds an extra layer of cover.

are beyond your control (weather, traffic jams, and other acts of God), there are things you can do to maximize the success of your stationary surveillance. The key is to think like a sniper. Think long-range and concealment.

1. DISTANCE

In stationary surveillance, distance is your friend. You want to go to Luigi's Restaurant for Lovers to catch your cheating husband, but, obviously, you don't want him to see you. Aim for maximum distance—the farther away you are, the less obvious you become and less chance you have of being detected. I've seen professional investigators camp out right outside a target's door. I'm thinking, *You guys are idiots. Even though you have a car with tinted windows, you're still a bunch of morons.* You always want to go down the block and away from the scene, as far away as possible, to observe a target. Remember, you have binoculars with you, so you have the tactical advantage of magnification.

FIVE WORST SURVEILLANCE OUTFITS

1. Hawaiian shirts: Busy, busy, busy!
2. Sports jerseys, unless your stakeout is in a sports arena: In some cities, wearing the wrong sports jersey is enough to get you into a brawl!
3. Low-cut shirts or miniskirts: I'm talking to the women—and some of you men—out there!
4. Sequins or anything glittery: Save it for New Year's.
5. Branded merchandise with large logos: You don't want to wear anything that is begging to be read.

2. CONCEALMENT

During a stakeout, the idea is not to be seen, which is why you want to put as much distance between you and your target as possible. However, even though you're far away, you should still try to hide or conceal yourself:

- Sit in the backseat of your car, preferably a minivan or an SUV that has tinted windows.
- Even if your car has tinted windows, carry a piece or two of black construction paper. Trust me, people are nosy and like to come and stick their faces against the glass if they think they see someone in a car. So when you see somebody snooping around, just hold the paper right up, and all he'll see is black. He won't see past it. Or you can tape black garbage bags to the side windows. That works too.
- Place your folding sunscreen in the front window, leaving a little crack so that you can view the action through binoculars or shoot photographs.
- Close the sunroof and make the interior of the car as dark as possible. Remember, the idea is to hide, because if people see you, you're done.
- Face your car away from the target, which gives the illusion of

disinterest, and watch through the back window. Or use a video camera to zoom in to a side or rearview mirror.

OBSTACLES

If you don't have the luxury of a vehicle for a stationary surveillance, you can make use of your surroundings and any available obstacles in order to conceal yourself from your target. These include another vehicle, a pole, a bush—anything that will hide you, and still afford you the opportunity to watch him.

If you have no recourse but to stand out in the open, try to blend in to your environment. Lean on a telephone pole. Try to look like you're doing something leisurely—reading a newspaper, sitting idly on a park bench, playing a game on your smartphone, looking at your watch as if waiting for your wife to come out of her office building. Just don't stand there aimlessly or else you might as well have a neon sign on you that reads, *Stakeout in progress*.

MONITORING A VEHICLE

Sometimes, if you have to disrupt or leave a surveillance, for one reason or another, and return at a later time, you might want to know if a vehicle has moved in your absence. You can mark tires. (Just be careful that you're not trespassing on private property and that the vehicle is parked on a public street.) Here's how:

- **Use a rock:** If you want to know whether a person has left a particular location and returned, you can place a rock—any rock you find on the street will do—at the top of the back tire. Come back later to see if it is still there. If it isn't, you'll know the vehicle has moved. (On a cold day, you can also check to see whether the vehicle's hood is warm.)

- **Use chalk:** Draw a chalk line from the tire to the street—it will look like an *L*. If the vehicle has moved while you were gone, the line on the pavement and the line on the tire will no longer meet. This trick's a little more obvious—the subject may notice that his tire has been marked with chalk, whereas nobody really pays attention to a small rock.

- **Use a watch:** My favorite way to mark a tire is to buy an inexpensive watch—a kid's watch—at Kmart for three or four bucks. Get something black, not shiny or brightly colored. Cut the band off, and set it to the proper time. Place the watch underneath one of the tires on the passenger side of the vehicle—not the driver's side, because the target might see it. If the target moves his car, he will back over the watch and break it, stopping the clock and locking in the time. Later on, when you recover the watch, you'll know exactly what time the target left the surveillance area.

THE CITY LOUSE AND THE COUNTRY LOUSE

As a private investigator, I conduct stationary surveillances across the country and have to fine-tune each one based on the environment I find myself in—city, suburb, or rural community. We had a lady once who lived on a main road out in the Long Island suburbs. She was an expert at insurance fraud—she committed it fifty times. Because she said she couldn't leave her house, we were hired to do a stationary surveillance. The problem was, though, that we couldn't just sit outside and watch, because there was no parking in the area. We run into that a lot in the suburbs. However, we discovered there was a trailer park development on this country road behind a wooden picket fence that had knotholes in it. We found a part of the fence with a nice-sized hole in it and stuck our telephoto lens through, so we could zoom in and watch her front door.

The idea is to find a faraway spot for yourself where you are concealed and where you can see. That can be real difficult when you get into rural surveillance, unless you dress like a cow in the field. There are also private property issues, because people have acres and acres of land and you can't trespass.

We had another job where we were watching an investigator for the New York State Police. He was a New York State Trooper

STATIONARY SURVEILLANCE BY ENVIRONMENT

	City	Suburbs	Rural
Distance:	Short distances	Moderate distances	Long distances
Concealment:	Easy to blend	Somewhat easy to blend	Difficult to blend
Obstacles:	Many	Some	Few
Obstacle types:	People, poles	Fences, shrubs	Trees, tall grass
Colors:	Blacks, grays	blacks, grays, browns, greens	browns, greens

detective, and he was out on disability. He lived in a cul-de-sac in New Windsor, New York. How do you watch a guy who's used to watching people? You really have to get tricky. In this instance, we went on this mountain road and set up between two houses. From there, we were able to see all the way down to his residence. So we're sitting up there and watching him, videotaping him. The guy's chopping wood. He's doing all sorts of stuff. Busted. Sometimes you can't watch them from one place, so you've got to watch them from another. You have to get crafty. It's almost like a game of chess. What piece can I move and not get taken?

THE USE OF DRONES

From time to time, particularly in rural areas or in the suburbs where there are big expanses of private property, I've employed surveillance drones, or unmanned aerial systems, to assist me in a stationary surveillance. Drones are already being used by law enforcement in many areas of the country, and they can carry all kinds of equipment—including live-feed video cameras, recording cameras (like GoPro), infrared cameras, heat sensors, GPS, and radar—that are helpful to private investigators.

Drones are available to anyone. You can buy them for anywhere between a few hundred to a few thousand bucks, and they can generally fly up to a thousand feet. Most batteries—on a decent unit—last about thirty minutes, so we usually have several batteries that are constantly on charge. We throw the drone up, and it becomes an observation post at about 200 or 300 feet. From there, we can see from a great distance, almost like a Secret Service helicopter in the sky. Even in high winds, the drone maintains its position.

Basically, drones allow me to get access to views that I wouldn't normally be able to get. For example, we once had a surveillance on Fire Island in New York. The client wanted to see if her husband was drinking or utilizing drugs, because there was a custody battle going on and if he got caught he would forfeit custody. He had a deck on this big oceanfront house—pretty wealthy guy. The beach near his house was public, so we went there one night. The guy was having a party. You really couldn't see what was going on from the ground, because the party was on the deck above, so we flew the drone up and were able to watch from the drone.

However, use drones with caution. Currently, there aren't a lot of laws surrounding drones, but the legislation is catching up fast. You don't want to be the test case. Remember, the same trespassing laws apply to drones as they do to feet, so you can't fly a drone over somebody's backyard just as you can't cross a property line on the ground. Use common sense.

MOVING (OR ROLLING) SURVEILLANCE

Sometimes your target doesn't stay in one place. Those cases call for moving, or rolling, surveillance, also known as *shadowing* or *tailing*. Moving surveillance is just what it sounds like—surveillance conducted on the move. Common methods include walking, driving an automobile, riding a bike, or traveling by airplane, cab, or train.

Moving surveillance is more of an art form than a science. It's like flying with no instruments as a pilot and by the seat of your pants. You have to know when to pull up so you don't hit the mountain, and you have to know when to go down and fly under the bridge. It's fluid, and conditions change second by second. There's a bus pulling out and about to cut you off. There's an old lady who's going to step off the curb. The traffic signal's about to change.

MOVING
SURVEILLANCE ESSENTIALS

Bring along all of the stakeout essentials when you conduct a moving surveillance, and add the following:

- **Full tank of gas.** Anything can happen. You might think it's just another day at the office for your target, but he jumps on the thruway and ends up in Canada.
- **Battery jump starter/inverter/compressor.** The last thing you need is car trouble.
- **A jack or a can of Fix-a-Flat.** The second-to-last thing you need is a flat tire.
- **E-ZPass.** If you're following your target on the highway, and he rolls through the E-ZPass toll lane, you don't want to get stuck in the cash lane, or else hasta la vista, baby!
- **Backpack or other carrying case.** For changes of clothing, maps, money, etc.
- **Sunscreen.** Whether you're on foot or in the car—some UV rays penetrate glass.
- **Comfortable footwear.** High heels are not conducive to moving surveillance.
- **FareCard.** You'll need one if you're following a target in the city, just in case he uses public transportation.
- **Cash or credit card.** If the target hails a cab or goes into a movie theater, you've got to be ready.

There's road construction, and now everybody has to merge. You can't predict all the factors in moving surveillance, so be prepared for everything.

IN THE CAR

When you tail someone by car, you have an extra layer of cover, but you are also at the mercy of the traffic gods. As with other types of surveillance, you'll want to maintain a comfortable

RUBBER BAND MAN

When following a target by car on a residential or city street, it's helpful to employ a rubber-band strategy. If I'm following you, I can't be right behind you. You'll see me. I'll get burned. I've got to give you at least a half-block lead. However, once you come to the corner, I've got to get much closer to you, because if I stay a half-block distance behind, and you turn right and then left, I won't know which way you've gone by the time I get to the corner. So the idea is to give distance on straightaways and then at areas where decisions can be made, you get much closer. Keep in mind that you'll probably kill your gas mileage, because you're going to be constantly on your pedal.

distance between you and your target, but this is easier said than done, because conditions are constantly changing.

Try to have as many vehicles as you can between you and the target, so that you can still see him, but he can't spot you unless he's looking for you. Sometimes that means following from a different lane, if you can, although it depends on where you are driving. If you're on a stretch of highway where you know there's no exit for the next six miles, you don't have to be up the guy's butt. You can watch him from the next lane. You can let a car come between you. Sometimes, if you have a friend with you in another car, you can sandwich people in: You and your friend can take up positions behind and in front of the target to control his speed. That works well on one-lane roads. Moving surveillance is a constant game of push and pull.

What if the target is doing eighty miles per hour on the highway? People are crazy. Sometimes we follow housewives who drive like nuts. They run red lights, don't stop for stop signs, make U-turns where it clearly states *No U-Turns*. (Bear in mind that a target's erratic

QUICK TIP

Put the sun visor down while you're driving behind a target. It will help conceal your face if he happens to glance in his rearview mirror.

I THINK I GOT BURNED BUT I'M NOT SURE

Sometimes, during a surveillance, you'll notice a new pattern to your target's routine. She's changing the way she goes to work. She's using a different subway line. Or she keeps glancing behind her. You might be burned, but you're not sure. I would advise that you keep going and try changing your look: At the next corner, where there's usually a crowd waiting for the light to change, step behind the tall basketball-player-looking guy, and reach into your backpack for your baseball cap. Put it on while you're looking between his armpits at your target, and turn your jacket inside out if it's reversible. Once the crowds start moving again—voila!—your target is looking for a guy with long blond hair in a black jacket, and you're now a guy with a baseball cap in a white jacket.

driving—speeding, constantly switching lanes, disobeying traffic devices—may be a sign that she's aware that she's being followed. She's looking to see: *If I do this, will that person do it too?*) You have to be careful. You can't drive recklessly even though the other person is driving recklessly. You could injure or kill somebody following a kook like that. My advice is to back off. Sometimes you have to live to fight another day.

ON FOOT

The same rules apply to moving surveillance by foot—distance, concealment, be safe. Crowds, in particular, can pose a problem when you're following a target through a swarm of people. If you go to Times Square in Manhattan during Christmastime, you literally almost have to be hanging on to the person's belt not to lose him. Or if you go down in the subway with him and you're not right behind him, subway doors can close before you get a chance to get on the train.

You can *never* take your eyes off a subject in a crowded city.

I, Spy

PUBLIC TRANSPORTATION

If you're on a bus, train, or subway car:

- Sit in front of the target. Let her look at the back of your head or try to sit sideways, so you can keep an eye on her.
- If you have a hood, put it on.
- Don't sit too close, but close enough so that the target can't leave through another exit without you noticing and following.
- If people get on and obstruct your view, you have to move. You can't assume that the target is going to get off on Thirty-Fourth Street, because that's what he does every day. You might get off at Thirty-Fourth Street and the guy is gone.

Never. I have agents who've said, "I looked away for a second, and he was gone." Moron, you took your eyes off the target! In a split second, the guy can go into a store or duck into the subway, and then you're done. I'm telling you now, people look the same from behind. It ain't easy. Try it. Go to Manhattan or Chicago or San Francisco during rush hour on a crowded street, and try following someone. Unless you're walking on Forty-Fifth Street in Manhattan between Eighth and Ninth Avenues, where there are row houses and really no place for the guy to go, the target is practically going to feel your breath on his neck.

BIKING IT

Sometimes, if they have a hard time keeping up, our agents will use a bicycle for a foot surveillance. Just because the target is walking doesn't mean you have to. You can rent a bike, or just know where your city's bike stations are, so you can grab one if you need it. It's cheap enough. (Also, bring a bike helmet and a lock in your backpack, in case you've got to lock the bike up to a pole or something.) Bikes give you a speed, stamina, and maneuverability advantage—you won't get as tired. I had one agent who used to do surveillance in the city and had one of these motorized Razr scooters. He was doing surveillance on a guy's wife who was a very, very big Central Park person, and she would jog. Try to keep up with a girl who's jogging when you're not a jogger . . . you're going to drop dead. I would always have the guy either go in with a bike or have one already there, chained to a pole, on standby. Just in case.

Outside of the city, mobile surveillance is a lot less intense. You can lengthen the distance between you and your target, slow down the pace. If the target goes into a restaurant, you can go in after a few minutes and sit at the bar and have a drink—just make sure you know how many exits there are in the place. Same with a hotel. If you're doing solo surveillance, you may have to take a position between two exits, and watch the elevator bank. Be prepared: Hotel security may come and ask, *What the hell are you doing here?* It's an issue. A lot of times, we'll have to check in to the hotel just to be able to hang out in the lobby.

PRACTICE MAKES PERFECT

At one time or another, you're going to lose your target. It happens to everyone, newbies as well as seasoned professionals. Sometimes, my clients have a hard time understanding. *How did you lose the subject?* I tell them that if you've never conducted a moving surveillance, you don't know how hard it is. You have to feel it. You have to learn it. You have to practice. As far as I'm concerned, you're never off duty. That's how you hone your skills. One night, while you're driving home from work, pick a target. Say, *I'm going to stay with the red Volvo in front of me.* If the guy switches lanes, switch lanes. If he gets off at the next exit and it's not your exit, let him go and pick another target. Practice staying with a subject and looking and anticipating what's going on around you: *Well, if this guy pulls out, he's going to cut me off. I better change lanes now and get in front of him.* You really have to train for physical surveillance as if you were running a marathon. You can't just wake up one morning and think, *Let me go follow my husband.* You have to get yourself prepared. You have to use common sense. And remember: if at first you don't succeed, eat your Wheaties and try again tomorrow. ■

EYE IN THE SKY: ELECTRONIC SURVEILLANCE

For most of us, our entire lives are stored on our computers—our work, our address books, our photographs, where we've been, where we're going, our likes, our dislikes, *our secrets*. Technology has become vital to how we function, but in accepting its convenience and ease of use, we've also have given up a lot of privacy. Smartphones, tablets, laptops—they're great. So great that we tend to forget that they all have the capability to track us and, with the right software, expose us.

For the art of surveillance, technology has been a godsend. Before GPS was around, we licensed private investigators were running around like chickens without heads. Follow that cab. Follow that woman. This way. That way. I knew a guy who owned a company that produced Caribbean frozen foods—you know, Jamaican beef patties and stuff. Somebody told him his drivers were picking up product from another warehouse and selling them out of his trucks along with the jerk chicken. We spent weeks doing physical surveillance on those guys, every which way. GPS would have saved us the trouble.

Electronic surveillance is the observation and gathering of information—usually on the sly—with the aid of electronics, such as cameras, microphones, and digital recorders, among other devices. There are two main reasons you would want to employ electronic surveillance on a case instead of performing a physical surveillance:

1. You *can't* physically be at a location. Lots of times, monitoring needs to take place in cramped, private quarters—often indoors—where private investigators don't have access to public areas and would stick out like a sore thumb.
2. You *don't want to be* physically at a location. Maybe, like in the beef patty case, there are too many people to track at once, necessitating many investigators, many miles, and many dollars spent.

Electronic surveillance has many applications:

- For business owners who want to make sure their employees aren't slacking off or stealing product or money.
- For mommies and daddies who believe their nannies are up to no good or possibly mistreating their child.
- For people who have elderly parents at home and want to check in on them to make sure they haven't fallen and can't get up.
- For home owners monitoring property, both inside and out.
- For pet owners who want to monitor their furry friends while on vacation or away from home. Those who follow me on social media know Harley, my maltipoo. When Harley hangs out at home, I like to check in on him from time to time.

THE RULES OF ELECTRONIC SURVEILLANCE

Like physical surveillance, electronic surveillance brings with it its own set of rules and laws by which you have to abide.

PERMISSION

You've got to have permission or the legal authority to perform electronic surveillance. My wife, Barbara, has a best friend named Sheri, and they both use Find My Friends, which is a free app that allows you to easily locate your friends and family using your iPhone, iPad, or iPod Touch. (It's also great for monitoring kids: *Where's my son? Did he come directly home? My daughter's missing, where the hell is she?*) They love it. They have agreed to track each other, so Barbara knows if Sheri is at the supermarket, the car wash, the post office. She knows everywhere she goes. Now, if they hadn't had this deal, and Barbara were to surreptitiously load the app onto Sheri's phone one day while Sheri's in the bathroom peeing, Barbara has now crossed the line into eavesdropping or invasion of privacy, which are both punishable crimes.

Remember, ignorance of the law doesn't excuse you from it, so you have to know what you're getting into when you perform an electronic surveillance. Curiosity sometimes really *can* kill the cat. When in doubt, consult with an attorney, because laws change all the time. It's cheaper to pay a little bit of cash to an attorney now to get that advice than to pay him to get you out of jail or a civil suit.

P.I. GLOSSARY

Eavesdropping: To overhear, record, amplify, or transmit any part of a private communication of others without the consent of at least one of the persons—or, in some states, both of the persons—engaged in the communication. **Invasion of privacy:** The intrusion into the personal life of another private person, without just cause. This can give the person whose privacy has been invaded a right to bring a lawsuit for damages against the person or entity that has intruded.

OWNERSHIP

Another way to think of permission is to think of it as ownership. If you're looking to install tracking software onto a computer or a telephone, ask yourself: Who owns this device? If the answer

DID YOU KNOW?

Laws on recording audio vary from state to state. For a state-by-state guide to recording phone calls and in-person conversations, visit the Reporters Committee at www.rcfp.org/reporters-recording-guide. Although the website is designed for journalists, the information applies to private investigators as well. If you're still not sure, consult an attorney.

is you, you're good. If the answer is your husband and he has given you permission, you're good. If the answer is the guy down the block, who has legally contracted with you to perform electronic surveillance, then you're good too. If the answer is your unsuspecting mother-in-law, then you're not so good.

AUDIO SURVEILLANCE

Audio surveillance is particularly tricky. Telephone recording laws govern the civilian recording of telephone conversations. (Recording by the government or by law enforcement, also known as wiretapping, is usually covered by specific laws.) According to federal law, at least *one party* taking part in a call must be notified of an audio recording, but there are some states that require that *all parties* consent to the recording of a telephone conversation. That's why businesses in all-party-consent states will announce that a call or a business interaction is being monitored—to train staff, for quality assurance or security purposes, etc. That's why you might see a sign that reads *Audio recording in progress* when you walk into Dunkin' Donuts in the morning for your bagel and coffee. They have to tell you. It's the law. Plus, those signs are actually a good crime deterrent.

So what does this mean for the Citizen P. I.?

- It means that if you live in an all-party-consent state, you can't be recording your conversation with your husband at the dinner

FIVE PLACES

WHERE YOU ABSOLUTELY, POSITIVELY CAN'T PUT A SECURITY CAMERA

- House that is not your own
- Changing or dressing room
- Bathroom stall
- Public place, like a park
- Sports locker room

table—even if it is taking place within a home that you own. If you really need to record that conversation, you have no recourse but to come clean and say, "I'm going to record this conversation."

- It means putting a recorder in your brother's car is illegal if you're not present, whether it's a one-party-consent state or an all-party-consent state. You're not there. No go.

VIDEO SURVEILLANCE

Thousands of business and home owners utilize video surveillance for the purposes of catching criminals, thwarting spouses, or monitoring loss prevention. For the most part, security cameras are legal in the United States as long as they don't intrude upon a person's right to privacy.

More and more people are employing surveillance cameras to keep an eye on family members, employees, and household help including babysitters, nannies, and other caretaker. Newer technologies are making it easier to slip these cameras into inconspicuous places throughout a home or business.

FIVE PLACES TO TUCK A SECURITY CAMERA IN YOUR HOME OR BUSINESS

- Teddy bears
- Clocks—go cuckoo for cameras!
- On a shelf with knickknacks
- Wall paintings
- Houseplants

Video surveillance can be a very powerful tool in crime detection and can ensure safety in the workplace while protecting your assets. You can monitor your entire business—every room—with a multi camera system to make sure your employees are not fooling around, or you can use a single unit to focus on vulnerable areas—a safe, a cash register, or even a specific suspicious employee. And weatherproof outdoor security cameras can help you keep an eye on the outside of your business and cut down on vandalism and property damage.

Today's cameras are easy to install and operate. Many video surveillance systems rely on the cloud, allowing you to access recorded or live video 24/7. All you really need are electrical power, a wireless Internet connection, and a downloaded app or software program to be used with your smartphone or personal computer. I have wireless cameras both in my home and in my business. There's one in my living room in my house, because Harley usually hangs out on the black couch, and in various offices and rooms of the International Investigative Group. If I get an

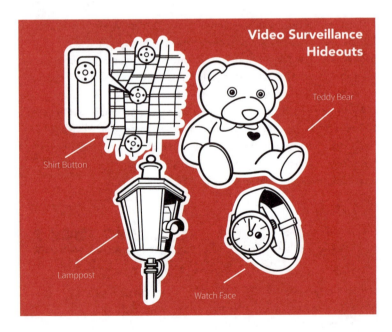

Video Surveillance Hideouts

Teddy Bear

Shirt Button

Lamppost

Watch Face

ARE YOU BREAKING THE LAW?

- You want to track your sister to be sure she is going to her college classes, and you put a GPS on the car she's driving—a car that's not in your name. **You're committing a felony!**
- You suspect your husband is having an affair, and you want to record his phone conversations while he drives to work, so you put a digital recorder in his car (a car that you may or may not own). **You're committing a felony!**
- You're in a one-party-consent state, and you surreptitiously put a recording device on a three-way office conversation that you're taking part in, and then you leave the conversation to see if the other parties talk about you. **You've committed a felony!**
- You bug your husband's cell phone to see if he's having an affair with his personal trainer. **You've committed a felony!**

alarm in the middle of the night, I can go to the app on my phone and see what's going on. During the day, if I'm out of the office, I can check on my employees and make sure they're working.

Also, in my line of work, security cameras come in pretty handy when I'm accused of misdoing. If someone tells me, "Hey, your daughter took a payoff from my husband when she did his lie detector test" or "My wife gave you oral sex to pass her in the poly room," I've got everything recorded and I can always go back to it.

When I perform a polygraph, I always ask for legal authorization: *I authorize video and audio recording of the entire procedure.* It means *Hey, I audio- and video-record everything, people, so don't try anything.* Unfortunately, people rarely read these things. Sometimes I polygraph someone, and he gives me an admission—*Yes, I did molest that child.* Great. Done. Take him away. But when he gets to *The Steve Wilkos Show*, he says, "Dan never asked me that question." I can go out on stage and say, "Steve, I've got it right on tape that I asked him this question." Let's go to the videotape!

HE SAID, SHE SAID

People often come to me for video surveillance when they're having marital problems. In the old days, a husband or wife would move out when a couple was on the verge of divorce. Today, we don't, because if you move out, you can lose rights to the house and can't come back in. So people are forced to live together and they're killing each other:

- "I want to know if he's coming in my room to search stuff."
- "My husband is trying to set me up and have me arrested for domestic violence, so he gets in my face and wants me to hit him."
- "My wife is trying to turn my kids against me."

Video can be a powerful tool in a court of law. With a camera, you can say, "Hey, officer, come on in and take a look at the camera footage. I never did any of that." As with audio, though, be sure you have permission and the right to use video surveillance. Check your local laws.

SPYWARE

Spyware is software that is installed on a computer and gathers information about a user's browsing habits, intercepts personal data, and transmits this information to a third party, which, as a private investigator, is you.

Businesses use all kinds of spyware. As an employee or visitor to a business, you really should have no expectation of a right to privacy when using an employer's computer. I've told my employees that all their computer work is being monitored. I mean, I have nice women working for me, but are they giving out secrets? Are they doing anything they shouldn't be doing? If you work for NBC, and you start sending out e-mails or watching porn, the company is going to know about it. It's not your computer, and you don't really have the right to do that.

Let's say you have a family computer, and you have children.

NINE WAYS COMPANIES MONITOR THEIR EMPLOYEES ELECTRONICALLY

- Internet usage monitoring: Have you been on Facebook all day?
- E-mail monitoring: Are you picking Fantasy Football teams on your company's dime?
- GPS: Are you snoozing in the park when you're supposed to be working your route?
- Keylogging: Why haven't you touched a single key on your keyboard in the past hour?
- Biometric (fingerprints, DNA, facial recognition): Do you have authorization to be in here?
- Audio recording: How many times are you going to call your girlfriend, pal?
- Video recording: I know the guy is cute and all, but are you going to stand at his cubicle and giggle all day?
- Security entrance log-ins and log-outs: What is that piece of hardware hidden under your raincoat?
- Copy machine monitoring: Is your butt really that big?

You want to install spyware to make sure that your fifteen-year-old is not texting with some molester online. That's perfectly acceptable—minor children don't have that expectation of privacy or their rights to privacy. This also applies to computers that are located in your children's rooms, if you've purchased them. It's your computer, and your children use your computer under your supervision—like an employee at a business.

Sometimes there are confidentiality issues—maybe your husband or wife is a doctor or lawyer or is working for a government agency. You can't really monitor stuff that's going to be confidential. Or if your husband buys a laptop for work, and you install spyware, you've got a problem. It's not your computer—or his, for that matter. There are gray areas, but, of course, when in doubt contact an attorney for advice—always the best thing.

MONITORING BY PHONE

There are all kinds of cell phone monitoring software, or you can use cell phone locators that are designed to help you track lost phones but can also help you monitor the whereabouts of your family members or employees. A lot of companies issue smartphones and tablets to their employees so they can track them and know their movements. It's sort of like punching a time clock:

"Where'd you go today?"

"Well, I made fifteen stops at these delis."

"Are you kidding me, pal? You sat in a parking lot of a movie theater for four hours."

A friend of mine works for Miller Brewing. He's one of their promotional sales guys. They gave him an iPad. They said, "This iPad is going to track where you are"—they told him outright—"because we want to see what you're doing during the day. If you're not working in the office, I want to make sure you're not playing golf, I want to make sure you're not at the peep show." My friend asks me, "How do you turn that thing off?" I'm like, *Tom, try doing some work. . . .*

CALLER ID

Caller identification, better known as caller ID, is a great tool for keeping track of who is calling your home or business. The service allows you to identify the telephone number of a caller before answering the call. But what about when you want to make a call and not have your phone number displayed? Private investigators need privacy, after all.

Let's say you want to call your husband to see if he's really at work, but you don't want to call from any of your phones—house phone, cell phone, etc.—because he knows all your phone numbers and will know you're checking up on him. Caller ID spoofing, a service that allows a caller to masquerade as someone else by falsifying the number that appears on the recipient's caller ID display, is no longer legal—neither is e-mail spoofing (for more on *spoofing*, see Chapter 8). And you don't want to use the private number feature on your phone, because your husband isn't likely to pick up a private number. What do you do?

BURNERS

Burners are mobile apps that offer temporary, disposable phone numbers—sort of like a legal type of caller ID, because you're not sending electronically false information. (Google also offers phone numbers, but they're not as burnable.)

As an investigator, burnable numbers are very useful, because a lot of times I want to find out information about somebody and I want to probe. If I want to find out some guy's work history, I can call him using a burnable number and say, "I'm calling from *Who's Who* and we're doing a page on you for the Internet. It's free. Give me your employment history." If the guy answers the phone, and I'm convincing enough, he'll tell me everything I want to know. If I have to leave a message, the guy can call me back on the burnable number I give him—it's a real number. Eventually, after I get everything I need, I can burn the phone number, as they say, and it essentially becomes untraceable.

So now that you've gotten a burner and you've called your husband and discovered that he's not at work—the liar—you can burn that number you're using. Turn it off. Kill it. And get another number, like a disposable phone. Your husband can't really find out it was you. It's traceable, but you need a subpoena, or for law enforcement to issue a court order, in order to find out who had a burner number at the time that a certain call was placed.

Another example: Let's say you found a number in your husband's wallet, and you want to know if it's a girlfriend. You don't want to dial from your home or cell number, so you get a burner number and you call up and you say, "I'm a friend of John's." The phone number is not attributable to you, and you can dispose of it quickly. Ultimately, is it traceable? Yes, but not to the average Joe.

Keep in mind, though, that if you call up the authorities and say, "I'm going to bomb the subway system," they are going to find you. They're going to get a subpoena, they're going to trace the number, and they're going to get you. You're committing a crime. So you don't want to commit a crime while burning, because they will find you. You don't want to defraud anyone. You don't want to steal money. You don't want to make a threat or anything along those lines. You want to be able to use this for investigative purposes, so that—assuming you will get caught—you have done nothing wrong. Burners just add a layer of cover for you. Chances are if your husband calls up the authorities going, "Someone called me and now the number is not in service, and my wife doesn't have that number," they're probably not going to sound any alarms.

UNTRACEABLE PHONES

Another thing you can do when you want to place an untraceable call is to get yourself an untraceable phone. Go to Best Buy or any other electronics store and buy a Tracfone, a prepaid phone with no contract. When you place a call with a Tracfone, the general calling area of the call is known, but not the person who made the call, because the phone is not registered to anyone in particular. However, you have to be careful with how you purchase that Tracfone:

- You don't want to pay with your credit card. Pay with cash.
- You don't want to get caught on a surveillance camera buying it, so you're going to have to put on a wig, baseball cap, and sunglasses, and refrain from looking up at the cameras.
- You don't want your regular cell phone with you the day you buy it. (Remember, cell phones track you 24 hours a day.)
- You don't want your E-ZPass with you either. It tracks you too.

Remember, mistakes are easy to make. In this case, one mistake, and you're done.

ID-ING PRIVATE NUMBERS

Now, let's say—instead of you making the call—you're receiving calls from a private number at your home, and you suspect your wife has a boyfriend and that he's the one calling at all hours of the night (doesn't anyone sleep anymore?). She keeps leaping for the phone every time it rings. Is there a way to find out what that number is?

Yes, there is:

1. You can use a mobile app like TrapCall, which, for a fee, can unmask the caller ID of blocked and restricted numbers, blacklist harassing callers, and even record your incoming calls. There is no software to install, and it works on any mobile phone.

2. You can use an 800 number. Callers cannot block their telephone number when a call is placed to an 800 number; it basically strips caller ID and will always register the calling number. So now you need to have your wife's boyfriend call an 800 number and have that 800 number be accessible to you. How?

At the International Investigative Group, we have a series of fake 800 numbers that we use to intercept people's phone numbers. If I want information about you, I'll send an agent to your house when you're not home, and he'll hang a card on your door that says: *American Delivery Service. We attempted to deliver a package to you. Please call us to deliver.* I want to know when you're home. I want to know if you've moved. I want to know if you still live there. I want to get your cell number. I want to get your home number. When you get home, assuming you still live there, you'll probably see this card and think, *Hey, this guy tried to deliver.* You'll call me at the extension on the card, say, extension 2288—which happens to be my case number for you—and I can either have the call transferred through, or I can have it answered electronically: *Hello, you've reached American Delivery. I'm sorry, nobody's here. Please enter the extension number.* Whether you leave a message or not, you've plugged in your extension, and now I have your phone number.

So to find out if your wife's boyfriend is calling your house, all you have to do is find a service that will rent you an 800 number. There are plenty of them—you can get a voice over internet protocol (VOIP) 800 number for a couple of bucks a month. Then transfer or call forward your calls to the 800 number for the day, or the week, and all your calls will go there. If your wife's boyfriend calls the house thinking he's blocking his number from your caller

ID, the joke will be on him. Once the call rings through to the 800 number, you've got his number—bam!—even if he hangs up and doesn't leave a message. Just go to your 800 call log, and you can see who's called you. Anybody can do it.

Scary, huh?

If there's one thing to be learned about electronic surveillance, it's that if someone makes a point to identify you, or goes looking for you, whether it's an officer of the law, a private investigator, or a private citizen, chances are he'll find you. Nowadays, there's always a trail. Technology often gives people a false sense of protection, a layer of security that lets them hide behind avatars and aliases and makes them feel anonymous, impenetrable, and difficult to find. Little do they know that, just by using technology, they've made it *easier* to find them. ■

3

GO
GET 'EM:
HOW TO FIND
ANYONE ANYWHERE

Many of the jobs I get as a private investigator involve finding missing persons. Some of these persons *want* to be missing (scammers, runaway teens, deadbeat dads) while others really don't (college roommates, high school sweethearts, second or third cousins). The good news for a private investigator is that, either way, these people leave trails, whether they know it or not. Wherever they go, whatever they do, it's like they drop tiny bread crumbs—photos, signatures, registrations—that lead right to them. The key to finding those crumbs is:

1. Knowing where to look; and
2. Knowing how to piece them together.

If you can do that, you really can find almost anyone.

There are many reasons why you would want to locate a person:

- He victimized you, maybe stole your money or property, and you want it recovered.
- He is a relative or friend from whom you've become estranged, and you want to reconnect. Death in the family. War. Marriage. Job relocation. Travel. Illness. There are many reasons people lose touch with one another.
- He is an old classmate or relative and you have a school or family reunion coming up. Facebook and other social media have taken a lot of the legwork out of trying to round people up, but even in this technologically connected world people can be hard to find.
- Your spouse or partner has left or disappeared and cannot be located.
- Your son or daughter has run away from home.
- You're searching for your birth mother or the child you gave up for adoption.
- You need to find someone related to a surrogate court matter. For example, your grea-uncle passed away and didn't leave a will, and his estate went into probate. You need to locate your cousins—his children—who are entitled to a piece of the pie.
- Your ex-husband hasn't been paying his spousal or child support, and you need to find him in order to serve him with court papers that require him to get on the ball.
- You've just been diagnosed with a sexually transmitted disease, and you have to find your former lover to notify him or her.

TOP 5 DESTINATIONS OF RUNAWAY TEENS

- Parent's house (particularly if the mom and dad are separated or divorced)
- Friend's house
- Boyfriend/girlfriend's house
- Another relative's home (uncle, aunt, grandparent)
- Anyplace that they feel has people who "understand" them

IDENTIFIERS

When conducting research or a background check on a person, identifiers help distinguish whether or not you are looking at the right person. Some of the most common identifiers are:

- Middle name or initial
- Social Security number
- Date of birth
- Current address
- Previous addresses
- Spouse's name
- High school graduation year
- Name of employer

The more identifiers you have, the surer you can be that you have the person you're looking for and the easier it is to gain additional information. For instance, if you're looking for a Sonia Smith who graduated from Small Town High School in 1986, and you discover there is a Sonia M. Smith who graduated that year, you now know that Sonia Smith has a middle name that begins with *M*. And that information may help you pinpoint Sonia Smith's profile on Facebook.

The list goes on and on.

Tracking these people down is a game of common sense. It's about using your head and the sources that are available to you. The best way to find someone is to approach the task with a two-pronged strategy: an extensive online search coupled with tried-and-true offline tactics. Used in conjunction with one another, there's virtually no one you can't locate.

ONLINE RESOURCES

The Internet has an inexhaustible supply of resources—many of them free—to help you locate a person without leaving the comforts of home.

DID YOU KNOW?

If you put a person's name in quotation marks when conducting research in a Web search engine, you will limit the responses you receive to that person's name. For example, let's say you want to find Katie Mindy Johnson. If you simply type *Katie Mindy Johnson* into a search engine, you may get results for *Katie Smith* and *Mindy Johnson*, or *Katie Mindy* and *Henry Johnson*—all the results will feature the names you have entered, but not necessarily exclusively or in the order you desire. However, if you search for *"Katie Mindy Johnson"* your results will filter properly.

SEARCH ENGINES

What's the first thing we do when we want to find a good restaurant or the name of that actor who played in that movie that took place during World War II? We perform an online search. Search engines, such as Google, Bing, and Yahoo!, are powerful tools that have become part of our everyday experience. With only a name and the click of a button, they can help you track down all kinds of information—addresses, phone numbers, maps of residential and business areas, places of employment, and alma maters, as well as events your missing person has attended or will be attending. Search engines are comprehensive and easy to use, and are the first place I go when I want to find a missing person, even if my client claims to already have conducted an online search. Simply type the person's name into the search engine box, and scan the listings. Sometimes you're done before you've even begun.

FACEBOOK AND SOCIAL NETWORKING WEB SITES

One of the first search engine items listed when you conduct an online search for a missing person is usually a Facebook page or other social networking web site page. Social networking web sites—more commonly called *social media*—are all essentially the same: It's free to join and you acquire friends/followers to form an online social network through which you engage. Each site has different rules, however. For example, Facebook and Twitter allow you to follow pretty much anyone (Facebook requires you to *friend* a person in order to access private information, while LinkedIn requires permission just to connect). Also, social media may have different specialties or areas of interest; LinkedIn is more business-y, while Goodreads focuses on books and authors.

The great thing about social media for private investigators is that people *willingly* put their entire lives on these sites, giving you clues to their current identity and whereabouts:

- **Here's a picture of my son, Johnny.** Now you know this person has a son named Johnny.

- **Here's my dog, Rover.** Now you know this person has a dog.

- **Here's me at our company picnic.** Now you know this guy works for Prudential.

- *Phantom of the Opera* **is just about to start. This is my third Broadway show in two months!** Now you know this person is relatively close to Midtown Manhattan, since he or she goes to the theater often.

People just spit information out to you.

Facebook, in particular, is an effective tool and has helped just about all of us find and reconnect with old friends and family members. After I perform a Google search, the next thing I usually do when asked to find someone is check out Facebook to see if the person has a profile. Chances are, he or she does—Facebook has nearly a billion daily active users, so that person is bound to be there. *Somewhere.* If the person you're looking for has a very common name such as Jones or Jackson, you need to look very closely at your search results to make your ID. Look at the profile pictures, full names, locations, marital statuses—whatever is available to you—in order to identify your person. It

POPULAR SOCIAL NETWORKING SITES

- Blogger
- Facebook
- Flickr
- Foursquare
- Goodreads
- Google+
- Instagram
- LinkedIn
- Pinterest
- Tumblr
- Twitter
- Wattpad
- Wordpress
- YouTube

can be tedious, but you need to be thorough. You don't want to make any mistakes.

If you've narrowed down your search results but are still not sure you have the right person, you can try "friending" that person to see more information. The person may or may not accept, but it's worth a shot. Glance at the data that is available to you and then send a believable request: *Hi, Donna, remember me from Small Town High School? Your sister was friends with my brother! I see you're still into knitting. What a beautiful family you have! Would love to catch up!* Sometimes just being polite and enthusiastic will work wonders.

PROFESSIONAL WEB SITES

Many professionals—lawyers, authors, doctors, real estate brokers, Pampered Chef consultants, private investigators, you name it—have professional Web sites, either of their own or as part of a business or corporation. Web sites function essentially as an online brochure or catalog, letting customers or clients know about the business's corporate structure as well as the arrival of new products, upcoming events, special promotions, or any new services being offered—information that is also useful to the private investigator. There is much information to be gleaned from a business site:

- **Professional name.** The person you're looking for might do business under another name. If you see a head shot of an executive that you know to be the person you seek, but the name doesn't jive, your person might be using another name professionally. That may be helpful information in terms of tracking down assets or career paths.

- **Business mailing address.** Even if the person is using a post office box as a mailing address, you'll still have a city in which that PO box is located. The person is bound to pick up his or her mail once or twice a week. Conduct a stationary surveillance, and catch him with his post office box key in his hand.

- **Business telephone number/e-mail address**. There may be more than one, so just jot all of them down. Every nugget of information moves you closer to your target.

- **Head shot**. Although head shots aren't always current, a picture can be worth a thousand Internet searches.

- **Social media profiles**. Sometimes a professional Web site will do all the work for you and round up each and every social networking site in which your person participates. Look for the social networking sites' icons either at the very top or bottom of the Web site's homepage, or on any Contact Us pages.

- **Press/Media**. Many business Web sites showcase company mentions in local or national media. Read through the articles made available to see if your missing person is featured, quoted, or pictured. Trade publications and periodicals often are overlooked places where you can find a wealth of information. For example, if a photo of him at a cocktail party appeared in a newspaper article covering last year's Consumer Electronics Show in Las Vegas, there's a good chance he'll be headed back to Vegas for the next one.

- **Portfolio/Image gallery**. Portfolios or image galleries usually showcase the work of an individual. If the person you're looking for is an artist, for example, you may recognize several Chicago photographs in his recent work, so you can book a plane ticket to Illinois. Or maybe she writes a lot for a certain national magazine and you can contact her there.

- **Blogs**. Blogs are usually informal, conversation-style articles, like diary entries. They can be found on professional Web sites and also on social networking sites such as Blogger and Wordpress. Blogs can offer insights into a person's specialty or area of expertise, what he cares about or he finds interesting, and his current whereabouts, especially if it is a travel or vacation-oriented blog.

In general, professional Web sites give you a snapshot of a person that may be different from what you find on social media. All of us wear different hats—mom, dad, businessman, teacher, pet owner, piano player—so it's important to research the business side in order to understand how or where that person spends the majority of his or her workday.

P.I. GLOSSARY

Skip trace: Tracking down someone who has left—or skipped—town and whose last known address is no longer valid.

ONLINE DIRECTORIES

Remember the old days of calling directory assistance when you were trying to locate a person? Nowadays, these directories are available for free online. The most popular ones are:

- Whitepages.com
- Anywho.com

Plus, there are thousands of company and association (professional, alumni) directories that are searchable. If you know the person you're seeking is an architect, try the American Institute of Architects. She last worked for a lighting store in the Seattle area before you lost track of her? Try the American Lighting Association. There's virtually an association for every profession out there.

Additionally, besides the standard social networking sites such as Facebook and LinkedIn, there are many Web sites where people seek out likeminded souls, family members, or are just looking to find that someone special. You too can utilize these sites, but for the purposes of finding a missing person. A few examples:

- **Online dating sites.** Are you on Match.com or eHarmony.com? Well, if so, you are already conducting your own person search without even knowing it! Finding that *special* person is no different from finding a *particular* person. For example, if you can't seem to locate that scoundrel who skipped out on you last year with a handful of your best jewelry, there's a good chance he may want to do it again. And again. And for many of these sites, *looking* is free.

- **Genealogy sites.** Researching your family tree is another form of finding a missing person. Sites such as Ancestry.com, which is the world's largest family history resource, can help you. All you need is a name to get started. Ancestry.com offers a free trial, after which you will have to pay a membership fee.

- **Alumni sites.** Web sites such as Classmates.com and Reunion.com can be great sources if you know the high school and graduating year of the person you're trying to find. Again, these sites offer varying levels of access. Basic searches or levels of information are often free.

PUBLIC RECORDS

People are always surprised by how much information about them is available for anyone to see. Trust me, there's a lot. Public records include personal information, minutes, files, accounts, or other records that a governmental body—federal, state, city, etc.—is required to maintain and that, by law, must be accessible to scrutiny by the public. There are many types of public records available:

- Census records
- Court dockets
- Professional and business licenses
- Real estate properties, appraisal records, deeds
- Registered voter information

P.I. GLOSSARY

DOB:
date of birth
POE:
place of
employment

DID YOU KNOW?

Many of the public records companies out there, such as Intelius, that offer to help you find people have inaccurate information. That's because oftentimes they're pulling their data from outdated sources. Many obtain their information from what's called a *credit header search*, which consists of the basic information of a credit report—name, variations of name, current and prior addresses, phone number, date of birth, and partial Social Security number. (Same goes for mailing lists companies, which lift names from all kinds of databanks and subscriber lists. If a person hasn't left forwarding information, then the list can only track him up to a certain point.) Basic searches from these companies are often free, but you may need to pay for advanced searches. These services are a good place to start, but they're not reliable. I would advise conducting a basic search—whatever you can find that's available to you for free—and verifying and expanding upon this information with your own investigation.

- Sex offender registration files
- Marriage license records (in some states)
- Derogatory information: bankruptcy records, notices of default, judgment index, and tax lien information (claims on property to secure a debt)
- Fictitious business names (companies that are *Doing Business As* other companies)
- Civil records: Filings of civil cases, including lawsuits and divorce proceedings
- Criminal records (felonies, misdemeanors)

COURT RECORDS

In the United States, court dockets are records of proceedings in a court case and are considered public record. They vary widely from jurisdiction to jurisdiction in the type and detail of information that is available.

The Federal Courts use the PACER (Public Access Court Electronic Records) system to house dockets and documents on all federal, civil, criminal, and bankruptcy proceedings. Although PACER (pacer.gov) is officially available to the general public, it is said to be used mostly by practicing attorneys because the site is difficult for non lawyers to navigate and has a "paywall" that requires users to pay significant fees for the documents they download. (In response, a browser extension called RECAP improves upon the PACER experience by helping users build a free and open repository of public court records, and purports to offer a more user-friendly experience.)

On the state level, the National Center for State Courts (ncsc. org) provides access to the court records of nearly all fifty states. Additionally, there may also be state-specific Web sites. For example, in New York State there is a Web site called nycourts. gov that I use for access to the New York State Court System for criminal as well as civil court data. The site shows a variety of information, including cases that are open, when a defendant's next appearance is, who the judge is, who the lawyer is, and so on. So if your landscaper is a scoundrel and has scammed you, you can look up his name in your state court system Web site. Maybe he has judgments against him. Or maybe you find out that the person you're looking for sued someone civilly in 2013. If you can't find your guy, you can look up the guy he sued and get some dirt. This is how you start developing leads and build a case. You may find he's been charged with one count of fraud or charged with driving without a license, and that he has a court appearance on Tuesday at the county criminal courthouse. You can get a process server to go to that court and serve him when he arrives. Sometimes the key to finding a missing person isn't knowing necessarily where he is, but where he's going to be.

CRIMINAL RECORDS

Someone will come up to me and say, "Dan, I'm looking for my client. I'm a personal injury attorney, and this guy is suing the city because he slipped on a banana peel, and I can't find him." You

BACKGROUND
CHECK ROADBLOCKS

Maiden/married names. Many women change their name when they get married. Therefore, if you're looking for your high school BFF, it's likely that you won't find her under her maiden name, particularly in legal documents, unless she hyphenates or still uses it. Similarly, if you only know someone by her married name and she uses her maiden name professionally, she can be more difficult to find.

Name changes. Name changes are not only a problem with women, but with men. Anyone can legally have their name—first and last—changed. If the person you are trying to locate has changed his name, it will be more difficult to find him.

Middle initials. People may not be consistent in their use of middle initials or middle names.

Common names. Smith. Jones. Cohen. Hernandez. When you are trying to locate someone with a very common name, filtering results becomes difficult, and you will have to rely on other criteria to pinpoint your target.

---

know the first place I look?

Jail.

Many municipalities—cities, counties, states—have Department of Corrections Web sites that will allow you to conduct an Inmate Population Information Search. Or you can try the Federal Bureau of Prisons. All you need is a name. Some states, such as Florida, provide detailed information—aliases, height, weight, tattoos the inmate has, what he was arrested for, when he was released. There are even photos. Another good source is VINELink.com, which is an online version of VINE (Victim Information and Notification Everyday), the National Victim Notification Network. This service allows you to obtain up-to-date and reliable information about criminal cases and the custody status of offenders. Essentially, it's an inmate locator

DID YOU KNOW?

There's a way to find out if a recipient opened one of your e-mails?
A subscription service called ReadNotify allows you to track emails
and documents you send. You'll know:

- The date and time the e-mail/document was opened
- The approximate geographic location of the recipient
- A map of the recipient's location
- The recipient's IP address
- Any URL clicks that are made within the email
- How long the e-mail was read for
- How many times it was opened
- Whether it was forwarded

that gives you access without you having to visit every state
Department of Corrections.

REAL PROPERTY RECORDS

Sometimes it's helpful to see where people have lived in order to
find out where they are now.

In New York City, there is a database called Automated City
Register Information System (ACRIS; a836-acris.nyc.gov) that
allows you to search property records—you can browse by name,
parcel identifier (borough, block, lot), document types, transaction
numbers, etc. It shows deeds (sometimes the property is co-owned
and you may discover that your missing person is married or living
with someone) and satisfactions of mortgage. You can actually see
the scanned document and check signatures—does the one on the
check she gave you match the one on the deed?

OFFLINE RESOURCES

Once you've exhausted all avenues using your computer, it's time
to think beyond the computer screen and maybe even get out of
the house for a little while.

**QUICK TIP**

If you're trying to identify someone in a crowd, try yelling out the person's name and then hiding. One of my agents was on the station platform for the 7 Train in New York City during rush hour, trying to ID a target, and he wasn't one hundred percent sure it was her. Finally, he yelled, "Hey, Roberta!" and hid behind an iron beam. In a sea of heads, Roberta's was the only one to turn in his direction. Ha, made ya look!

DIRECTORY ASSISTANCE

I know virtually none of us dial 411 anymore, considering there is online directory assistance, but those operators are still around. If the online white pages turn up nothing, go old school and dial local directory assistance at (area code) 555-1212 from your phone. It's worth a try.

GPS

For cases of missing teens, friends, or spouses, you can take advantage of GPS technologies in order to find them, particularly if you've installed surveillance apps on their phones or in their cars (remember, to have done so, those items must have been purchased by you and must be in your name).

Years ago I was hired by a National Hockey League player to find his wife who up and left him one day with the kids. She just put them in the Escalade, drove off, and disappeared. However, because she was driving my client's vehicle—the Escalade was in his name—we were able to track her through OnStar, which provides subscription-based communications and in-vehicle security. We were able to call and say, "Listen, we're dealing with a parental abduction here in a vehicle that belongs to my client. You've got to tell me where this car is." OnStar ended up tracking her to North Dakota, which is where she is from originally. Not much of a surprise there. We had the sheriff in town serve her with court orders, what they call writs of habeas corpus, which instructed her to bring the children back to New York, and that was that. Case closed.

INFORMANTS

Most people think of Deep Throat when they think of informants—people meeting in a dark parking lot and kicking suitcases of confidential information across the pavement to each other. While the use of informants is usually not that dramatic, it can be just as effective. (We'll talk more about informants in Chapter 5 in relation to obtaining information or evidence from them when the whereabouts of a target are already known.)

Informants can be anyone from a close relative to a perfect stranger. Their one criterion is that they *know*—or at least you think they know—where your missing person is located. So how do you get an informant to snitch?

1. Money: Money is the universal enticement. Service workers, such as garage attendants, porters, janitors, and doormen, usually prefer money as an incentive. The CEO of a Fortune 500 company, on the other hand, is probably not going to give anyone up for fifty bucks.

2. Subterfuge: You can pose as any kind of believable occupation to find your person: a freelance writer working on a story (try not to attach yourself to any organization, because the informant can research you and catch you in a lie) or a representative from an alumni organization. Think of who *you* would provide information to, if asked, and become that person for the next half hour.

P.I. GLOSSARY

Asset: a person who provides information, such as a witness or an informant

One time, a very wealthy British hedge-fund guy hired me to find his girlfriend, a well-known television personality, who had taken his two Westies. He wanted those dogs back badly! He said, "These two dogs are my babies. I have no children. I'm not married. I want my dogs back. I don't care what it costs me." So I hung up the phone and said to my wife, "I'm Ace Ventura, Pet Detective, now." (Dogs are considered property, so, for example, if a couple were to divorce, whoever paid for the dogs gets them in the divorce agreement. This couple wasn't married, but the ownership papers belonged to my client.)

I contacted a family member under the pretext of trying to see if the girlfriend was interested in some TV work. The family member gave me her home number, which I traced to Denver, Colorado, where she had a condo. When my agent knocked on the door to her condo, she wasn't home, but he heard two dogs barking. I told my client, "We found them," and he wanted us to keep the place under surveillance. I explained that she probably wasn't going anywhere, since she was at her home and not a hotel, but the guy said, "I want you to watch that place with a twenty-four hour surveillance, so she doesn't escape with my dogs!" We wound up getting a judge's order from New Jersey, another habeas corpus—habeas dogus, I guess—that the local sheriff served on the girlfriend, and she wound up bringing the dogs back. Then the guy threw a welcome home party for his dogs on his fifteen-acre estate out in western New Jersey like you wouldn't believe!

3. A combination of money and subterfuge: Basically, if one doesn't work, try the other. Between slipping him the cash and

TWO **TYPES OF INFORMANTS**

- People who care for your missing persons and want to see them happy: relatives, friends
- People who despise your missing persons and want to see them get what's coming to them: angry friends, disgruntled employees

SETTING A TRAP

From time to time, you may have difficulty locating someone. You've exhausted all avenues or perhaps the person is out of the country and you can't get close enough or pinpoint exactly where he'll be and when. You can try setting a trap. In other words, you want to lure that person out of his place of comfort or hiding place and into a setting that you stipulate or control. You need to outfox the fox.

Currently, I'm trying to locate a guy who lives in Italy. We want to serve him with New York court papers because he's needed as a witness for a trial. The guy is extremely wealthy—a multibillionaire who owns several companies—and we are trying to get him when he travels to New York or to one of his companies in New Jersey or Pennsylvania, but we can never get a lead on the guy. He's a European citizen and travels in and out of the country on private planes and stays in exclusive hotels.

I decided to pretend that I was a freelance reporter who wanted to write an article about one of his products. I contacted him via his business e-mail address, which I picked up on his corporate Web site, and said I was interested in pitching the story to all the top newspapers—*The New York Times, USA Today, The Wall Street Journal*—in order to see who bites. Could he tell me when he would be in his office next for an interview? I was using his vanity, his desire for free publicity, against him. What businessman doesn't want free publicity?

I really sold it: *It doesn't cost anything. It could be great publicity for you, sir.* Yadda, yadda. You know, to butter him up. And there's nothing illegal about it. I wasn't defrauding him. I wasn't scamming him out of anything. I just wanted to set up an appointment with him at his office. Remember, sometimes you have to lie to find the truth. That's the premise of investigation. If it works, great. I'll get him. If it doesn't, I'll try something else.

your sob story, you've got a good chance of the informant complying.

PATTERNS/PROFILING

Like the hockey player's wife, people are usually creatures of habit, which makes them easier to find. They generally do what they like to do. She had a house in Colorado, so that's where we found her. If you want to find a person who likes to visit Disney World, you look for him in Orlando, Florida, because he's probably on the "It's a Small World" ride and not in Idaho. One time, we were hired to find a guy in his mid sixties who was involved semiprofessionally in horse racing. I asked his wife, "What does he like to do?" She said, "He loves horses and likes to go to the tracks in Florida." So we tracked him, and guess where he was? At a racetrack in Florida. You don't need to be a rocket scientist to figure that one out.

As you're compiling information from Web sites, friends, informants, and additional channels, look for patterns. Does this person prefer McDonald's over Burger King? Does he like to spend time at the library or at dance clubs? Where are this person's favorite places? Wherever that is, that should be the first place you look. He may not be there, of course, but it's your best shot.

If your missing person owns a house, votes, or pays taxes—and the vast majority of us do—he's going to be found. It's just a question of how much or how little this person has in his name that you can find; the more successful or accomplished you are, the more bread crumbs you leave. (Keep in mind that if you can get this information, the bad guys can too.)

Investigation is the art of collecting all those pieces of the puzzle—a photo from a Facebook page, a signature from a deed, a middle name or initial from an association page—and compiling a comprehensive profile, a life's worth of documents and dealings, that tells the story of a person. And that person can be anyone. Even you. ■

4

TRUE CRIME:
HOW TO TELL IF SOMEONE IS
LYING

Private investigation is the art of detection. Investigators spend much of their time physically tracking people down in order to expose their *whereabouts*. However, private investigation is also the art of exposing people's *characters*—are these people telling me the truth? Are they who they say they are? Can I trust them? What are their motivations? Are they going to rip me off? Cheat on me? Hurt my kids? Are they friend or foe? While private eyes are out there conducting subterfuge—lying, pretending—in order to achieve an objective, they're also trying to figure out whether others are doing the same to them.

P.I. GLOSSARY

Suspect:
a person thought to be guilty of a crime or an offense.

In the business, we refer to this as credibility assessment: a psychological detection of deception. It is the monitoring and evaluation of not only a subject's spoken words, but the way those words are spoken, the absence of them, the time it takes for a person to say them, and the facial expressions and body language associated with them.

Many types of people use credibility assessment, from law enforcement officers to mental health physicians and psychologists to juries, who, not unlike citizen private eyes, use it to determine a person's innocence or guilt. The techniques of credibility assessment are applicable to practically any situation:

- A woman confronting her husband who she suspects is having an affair.
- A parent having a talk with her teenage daughter, who she suspects has crashed the family car.
- An employer interviewing an employee after a coworker accuses him of slapping her butt at the water cooler.

Assessing credibility is something that we do on a daily basis. I will teach you to become better at it.

THE TRUTH IS OUT THERE

There are two main ways to solicit information from someone during conversation:

- Interview: An informal question-and-answer session. An interview may be performed with a suspect, a victim, or a witness to a crime (even if the crime is stealing cookies from the cookie jar).
- Interrogation: A formal and systematic question-and-answer session. The purpose of an interrogation is to elicit a confession from a person, often a suspect. You know the guy did it and you want him to admit it.

Both interviews and interrogations have certain procedural strategies:

SIGNS THAT YOUR SPOUSE MAY BE CHEATING

- They are more concerned with their appearance—e.g., losing weight, dyeing their hair.
- They have changed their style of dress or the perfume/cologne they wear.
- They are wearing different underwear.
- There is a change in intimacy level—they're either cutting you off from intimacy or being more intimate (because they feel guilty).
- They tend to guard or hide their phone.
- When you walk into a room, they appear startled and immediately change what they're doing—e.g., hang up the phone, switch tabs/pages on their computer screen, or shut down their computer entirely.

INTERVIEW VERSUS INTERROGATION

1. Interview

Goal: To gather information and perform a credibility assessment. Think of it as a fact-finding mission.

Tone/demeanor/body language: The tone of an interview is non accusatory. *We're just talking. Nothing to be alarmed about.* Subtly adjust the tone, volume, and speed of your voice as well as your body movements and gestures so that they *mirror*, or *match*, your subject's. (For example, if the subject uses hand gestures, use them too. If he has his legs crossed, cross yours too.) This will help to develop a rapport and make the subject feel more comfortable, which increases your chances of eliciting information. Even if you know a subject is lying to you or is exhibiting a clear indication of deception, play it cool. The goal is to keep the subject talking in order to answer your questions.

PRE-EMPLOYMENT
INTERVIEWS

By law, there are certain questions employers cannot ask a prospective employee. They cover:

- Sexual orientation
- Ethnicity
- Age
- Religious views
- Disability
- Children—whether you want them or have them
- Political affiliation
- Marital status

Location: Interviews should be performed in a neutral setting. An employee lounge. A living room.

Positioning: You and your subject should be comfortable, with ample room for each. However, there should be nothing between the two of you, so you can accurately gauge his body language.

Amount of speaking: During an interview, the investigator should speak 5 percent of the time. Investigators or law enforcement officers usually conduct what are called *narrative techniques*— they let suspects or subjects go on and on without interruption in hopes that they will say something incriminating or contradictory. Therefore, stay away from yes-or-no questions and try to keep your questions succinct: As far as your subject knows, you have no idea, for example, that he stole money from petty cash or scammed Old Man Jenkins out of his Social Security check, but if you reveal too much info in your line of questioning and he gets the slightest whiff that you're on to him, he'll clam up.

2. Interrogation

Goal: To persuade the subject to tell the truth or admit wrongdoing.

Tone/demeanor/body language: As with an interview, you want to begin with a non accusatory manner. Speak kindly, softly. Mirror and match their voice and body movement. For some subjects, you will continue like this throughout the interrogation.

DID YOU KNOW?

Some interrogation tactics are so persuasive that they can elicit a false confession. You can help avoid your subject copping to an offense he or she didn't commit by:

- Keeping interrogations short. No need for these things to drag on. After a few hours, even you may end up saying you're guilty.
- Making sure subjects are in a good state of mind. The best time to interview your daughter about exactly where she was last night is not when she comes stumbling through the door piss drunk at two A.M.
- Making sure your subjects are capable of understanding what you're asking. This usually applies to minors, who may admit to something if they think it will make their parents happy, and individuals who are not fluent in the language of the interview or interrogation.

You'll express understanding toward your subject's behavior, because, psychologically, it's easier for a subject to come clean when another person appears to identify with why he has done what he's done. For other subjects, you'll need to become incrementally more aggressive in order to elicit a confession. It's important to constantly gauge your subject and make adjustments based on his responses.

Location: Interrogations should be performed in a setting where the questioner or interrogator has the home-court advantage. Law enforcement officers will conduct interrogations in the lock up. In the civilian world, it might be the boss's office, the principal's office, or a dad's home office.

Positioning: As with an interview, there should be nothing— no desks or coffee tables—between you and your subject. During the course of the interrogation, you'll want to encroach incrementally on a subject's personal space; you want to lessen the distance between you. This will create a feeling of intimidation in the subject, a feeling that there is no protection and nothing to hide behind.

Amount of speaking: The investigator should speak for the vast majority—or approximately 95 percent—of the time. Also, there should be no accusatory questions, at least until the very end when you think your subject is ready to confess or tell the truth. Instead, think of an interrogation as a monologue or a presentation of a report—you are making statements, not threats, which are designed to persuade your subject to tell the truth:

1. Address the reasons why the interrogation is taking place—there is money missing from the petty cash box, an unexplained absence from school, or a new bruise on your son or daughter.
2. Present the evidence—a security camera image of your subject opening the petty cash box, witness testimony that your subject has been skipping school, or photos of welts on your child's face.
3. Make a logical or rational argument for the person's guilt. *I could see why you would want to steal … I was a teenager too, once … I know, parenting is difficult.*

TO TELL THE TRUTH

Human beings use the same subconscious strategies to deceive—certain words and phrases, sentence structures, and types of content. Whether the question is being asked to your child, your wife, a guy you met at a bar, a prospective employee, or a college professor, you want to listen to what a person says and how he or she says it. Years of research have identified the linguistic signals that differentiate deception from truth. Your job as a private investigator is to discern them.

1. Evasion
People who are guilty have a hard time saying no. Instead, they answer a question with a question or avoid the question altogether.

> Interrogator: "Did you ever commit a crime?"
> Suspect: "Do I look like somebody who would commit a crime?"

OMISSION VERSUS COMMISSION

Question	Commission	Omission
Are you cheating on me?	No, I would never cheat on you.	Please . . . I love you.
Did you inappropriately touch that child?	No, I didn't.	Is that what you think of me?
Are you drinking again?	Yes, I'm sorry.	Just because I'm late doesn't mean I'm drinking.

Interrogator: "Did you sexually molest that girl?"
Suspect: "Why would I molest a girl? I have a beautiful wife. I get all the sex I want."

2. Hesitance/latency and/or filler words

Delayed responses or the use of filler words or stall tactics—*um, you know, excuse me*—afford a subject more time to come up with a plausible lie. If a person doesn't answer your question with confidence and assurance, it should be considered a red flag. Law enforcement officers look for this kind of thing all the time in trying to detect probable cause for further investigation.

Scenario #1

Officer: "Excuse me, miss, what are you doing in this neighborhood?"
Suspect: "I'm going to see my grandmother. She's lived here forever. She won't move."
Officer: "What's your grandmother's name?"
Suspect: "Suzie Smith."
Officer: "Where does she live?"
Suspect: "123 Main Street, Apartment 8."

Officer: "What are you doing for grandma?"
Suspect: "I'm bringing her medicine from CVS.

This woman seems believable. There's no latency, no hesitation, and her story makes sense. Therefore, there's no probable cause. She appears to be telling the truth.

Scenario #2:
Officer: "Miss, what are you doing in this neighborhood?"
Suspect: "Why? Um, I'm . . . I'm . . . um, visiting my
          grandmother."
Officer: "What's your grandmother's name?"
Suspect: "Her name? Her name is . . . um, Sara."
Officer: "Where does Sara live?"
Suspect: "Oh, um . . . Over there in that building."
Officer: "What apartment?"
Suspect: "Excuse me?"
Officer: "I asked what apartment, miss."
Suspect: "You want the number? Wait, I can't remember the
          floor . . ."
Officer: "Would you mind stepping out of the car?"

This simple exchange produces probable cause for the officer to check this woman out. She is exhibiting clear signs of deception, and he has been trained to recognize them. I had a highway cop in my office one day. I was polygraphing his girlfriend, because he had strong suspicions that she was cheating on him. He goes to me, "I don't know why she didn't think I would know. I get lied to a hundred times a day: 'You were speeding.' 'I was? I didn't know I was speeding. This is a new car.' 'Sir, the car is four years old.'" Police officers know when something doesn't make sense.

3. Vague sentiments
Specificity is what innocence is made of. When a subject produces vague responses, it may be a sign of guilt or that he's not being truthful.

Officer: "Sir, what are you doing here in the middle of the night? You're walking a bit erratically."

Suspect: "Oh, I'm fine. I've got some stuff to do."

Officer: "Exactly what stuff, sir?"

Suspect: "You know, this and that."

Officer: "Can you be more specific, sir?"

Suspect: "Why you hassling me?"

4. Use of the word *honestly* or a similar phrase

Guilty people think that throwing out words such as *truthfully* and *honestly* is going to get them off the hook, but those words are often used as a decoy or stall tactic.

Husband: "Did you cheat on me?"

Wife: "Honestly? No."

Parent: "Did you hit your sister?"

Child: "Okay, Mom, this is the truth . . . I didn't do it."

5. Diverting blame

Kids do this all the time. It's so much easier to pawn off the guilt or responsibility on some unsuspecting sap.

Parent: "Joey, why did you flunk out of this class?"

Joey: "That class was ridiculous. The teacher was horrible. Ask anyone."

Employer: "I'm really impressed with your and Jerry's work, Jim. The only part that needs work is the second section of the report."

Employee: "Oh, Jerry mostly handled that section. I agree. It's not as strong as it could be."

6. Doth protest too much

If someone starts having a conniption just because you asked a simple question, it can be a tip-off to deception.

Girlfriend: "Tommy, did you make out with Melanie at Cody's house last night?"

Boyfriend: "What?! Who told you that? That person is a *liar*! I am going to get to the bottom of this. How dare someone spread these awful lies about me!"

7. Projection

In psychology, a projective test is a type of personality test in which a subject offers responses to ambiguous scenes, words, or images that are shown to him. (The most commonly known type of projective test is the Rorschach Inkblot Test.) The theory behind the test is that when someone is presented with clearly defined questions, his or her conscious mind will answer in clearly defined responses. However, if you present a question or stimulus that is not clear, underlying or unconscious motivations or attitudes take over and can be revealed. In other words, people project their real feelings when they can't focus on a desired result.

I perform these types of projective tests all the time in my office, and you can do it too. You don't need official cue cards, inkblots, or the like. Use what you have available to you—paintings on the wall or photos on your desk—as conversation starters. Ask the person to tell you what happens before the picture, what is happening in the picture, and what happens after the picture.

Conversation Starter

In general, I find that truthful people tell upbeat stories that make sense, while deceptive people tend to be more negative, and their stories lack an ending or don't make sense. For example:

TURNING
THE TABLES ON A SO-CALLED
TELEMARKETER

Scammers are looking for every opportunity to bilk you out of something, usually money. Even with the advent of Do Not Call lists, our phones still manage to ring off the hook from people looking for donations or offering us better finance rates on our credit cards. How can you tell if these people are for real? The best thing to do, as you'll read in Chapter 8, is to hang up the phone, and contact the organization or credit card company directly. However, you should also listen for those linguistic signals—hesitation (*I'm still here, ma'am, it's taking me a moment to pull that up*), repeating a question with a question (*Can you repeat that question, ma'am?*), or diverting blame (*I'm sorry, ma'am, our computers are down at the moment, and I don't have access to that information . . .*)—in order to help you validate their legitimacy.

- A truthful person might say:
  "Before this picture, a family wanted to sail on this beautiful day."
  "In this picture, they are sailing, and the waters are calm."
  "After the picture, they go back home, have a nice barbecue dinner, and drink some wine."

- A deceptive person might say:
  "Before this picture . . . I don't know . . . People wanted to move their boat before a storm hits."
  "In this picture, they are rushing to move the boat to get away from the storm."
  "After the picture, the boat gets destroyed by the storm anyway."

BODY OF EVIDENCE

Human beings communicate in learned nonverbal patterns—facial expression and body language—that present telling

DID YOU KNOW?

The study of nonverbal communication is called *kinesics*, which was originally brought to mainstream use in the fifties by U.S. anthropologist Ray Birdwhistell. He coined the term from the word *kinesis*, which is Greek for "movement".

indicators of deception. When people come to my office for a polygraph or an interview, I'm assessing everything they do the second they walk through the door. Are they looking me in the eye? Did they offer to shake my hand? Was their handshake firm? Did they keep their jacket on or take it off? Were they smiling? Were they smiling too much?

Bosses, teachers, parents—they should be doing the same kinds of assessments when conducting an interview or interrogation. They should be looking for that subconscious gesturing or what we call *leaking deception*, which, as you'll discover, becomes very obvious once you know what to look for. Of course, you should keep in mind that nothing in investigation is foolproof. Certain facial expressions and body gestures can be the result of mental health and cultural concerns, whether it's the inability to keep consistent eye contact or a coping mechanism that produces facial tics or foot tapping. That is why it is important to observe an individual both at rest and at stress. If the nonverbal cues begin only at the most crucial or most taxing moments of an interview or interrogation, then that is a pretty good indication of deception. Your best bet is to assess your subject using more than one, or a combination, of the following signs.

1. Fear. Sometimes when I get people hooked up to a polygraph, they look like they're going to pass out. Although they simply may be nervous, in a general way, about taking a polygraph, that's usually not a good sign of a person's innocence. This is known as *fear of detection*.

2. Eye contact. When it comes to discerning the truth, the eyes usually

SIGNS OF LEAKING DECEPTION

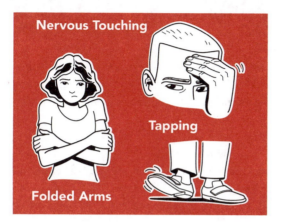

Nervous Touching

Tapping

Folded Arms

- Licking lips
- Fidgeting
- Self-soothing: rubbing legs or arms
- Distance (the subject puts distance between himself and the interrogator)
- Folded arms (the person is protecting himself)

- Runner's legs (bouncing knees, tapping toes)
- No eye contact
- Palms down
- Twitching
- Nervous touching of face
- Gulping

have it. Deceptive people generally don't look you in the eye or they break eye contact, particularly at the point of answering a question.

3. Fidgeting. Remember that expression *ants in your pants*? Well, deceptive people have a whole army of them in their underwear. They can't sit still or make themselves comfortable.

4. Touching parts of their face or body.
Deceptive people rub their face, their legs. Girls

will twirl their hair, also called *grooming*. If you ask your boss if you can have a raise, and he touches his nose while telling you, "There's no room for it in the budget," it may be time to look for a new job. Touching his nose while answering a question means . . . his answer stinks!

5. Fight or flight. Those old caveman instincts have stayed with us over the course of hundreds of thousands of years and seem to turn up at crucial moments of deception—when we feel backed into a corner:

> Father: "You stole the money."
> Son: "I did not steal the money. What are you talking about?"
> Father: "You did."
> Son: "That's it. I'm going to my room."

6. Distance or barriers. As I stated earlier, you never want to interview or interrogate someone across a table or a desk, because that gives him the perception that something is protecting him. And when there's nothing for a guilty person to hide behind, he will:

- Try to create distance between the two of you, by leaning back in his chair or physically moving a chair back.
- Use his body as a barricade to give the illusion of protection, such as folding his arms, or crossing or extending his legs.

Distance or Barrier Sitting

7. Charm. Flirting. Flattering. Buttering up the questioner. It's unbelievable to me that people really do this, but they do. As if telling me they like my hair or my watch is going to make me give them a gold star on their polygraph.

8. Joking. The minute some clown breaks into a story about a priest and a rabbi who walk into a bar, he's already dug himself into a hole. I'm the only one who should be making bad jokes in my office!

9. Inappropriate reactions. Sometimes during an interview or interrogation—and we get this often on *The Steve Wilkos Show*—a guest acts weird or in ways that are not congruous with the questions being asked. In the business of credibility assessment, we call this *unusual affect*.

> Questioner: "Did you sexually molest that girl?"
> Subject: "Hahaha! I wouldn't sexually molest a girl. That's funny."
> Questioner: "What do you mean it's *funny*?"
> When you enjoy something, when you enjoy the power, it will show.

GOING IN FOR THE KILL

During the course of an interrogation, you will reach a point of critical mass. Your suspect will be ready to crack. Some common signs of an impending confession include:

- Crying
- Putting her head on a table or a desk or in her hands, as if overcome by emotion
- Slumping in a chair, as if giving up or defeated
- Looking down and ashamed

That's when it's time to go in for the kill, and there are a variety of ways to do it:

DECEPTION IN WRITING

So much of our communication is done via writing, particularly through texts and e-mails. It is possible to detect deception in writing. Law enforcement officers and private investigators often employ what's known as Linguistic Statement Analysis Techniques (LSAT) that can detect lies in both spoken and written statements by focusing on word choice, structure, and content. Applying LSAT to a written statement is like subjecting someone to a polygraph examination. As with spoken interviews, it's all about what you say and what you don't say in your writing. Look for:

- All the spoken cues we've discussed—answering a question with a question, assigning blame, hesitation, etc.
- The use of fewer first-person pronouns. Deceptive people avoid statements of ownership and focus more on the actions/motivations of others.
- More negative emotion words. These include *hate*, *sad*, *bad*, *empty*, and *useless*.
- Change of language with relation to a specific person or item, usually the subject in question, such as calling a murdered child *Bobby*, then *my son*, and then depersonalizing him to *that boy*: *I took Bobby out to the woods to find frogs. My son really likes going into the woods. I lost sight of him, and later I found that boy face down in the creek.*
- Unimportant details take precedence: *I woke up and turned on the TV, but the* Today *show was not being hosted by the regular hosts, so I changed the channel and watched* Good Morning America *instead. Then I went to make toast and burned the first piece. It made a lot of crumbs as I took it out of the toaster, so I got a wet rag and cleaned the counter. I made another piece of toast and used butter, since I don't like margarine.*
- A delay in getting to the event in question and then rushing through the event with little or no detail, or never even saying what the event was.

- **Kindness.** You know the expression "You can catch more flies with honey than vinegar?" You can catch more lies too. When your subject is about to break, offer a soda or something to eat, and say, "Are you okay? I know this is hard." Kill 'em with kindness!

- **Empathy.** Explain that you've had the same feelings too. *Joe, I know that you stole the money from the safe, and I have to tell you something . . . When I was in my twenties, I did something very similar.* Your subject will get the feeling that what he did isn't so bad, because you did it too.

I recently interrogated a girl who worked for a doctor's office in Manhattan. She was stealing the cash deposits. All she did was complain to me that the doctor would make her pick up her personal dry cleaning and laundry. Instead of saying, "You're her personal assistant, you idiot," I said, "Listen, I understand. Some doctors take advantage of you. I see where you're coming from. I know. I had a boss who pissed me off once, and I stole money from his wallet. I felt awful about it. Listen, your boss isn't interested in prosecuting you. She just wants to get her money back. She understands you're a young girl and that you made a mistake. You are not a bad person. I know you did not mean to do it. Let's move forward from this." I got the money back. I got a signed confession. I got a separation agreement. All with empathy and kindness. Sugar, sugar!

- **Let the subject save face.** Tell her: "I know you've been raised as a good person. Your parents were hardworking people. We all make mistakes, and making a mistake, apologizing, and moving forward is what a good person does. You're a good person, right, Beth? I'm very proud of you. It takes a big person to own up to what she's done."

- **Ask leading questions.** This is a famous technique, the most common example being, "When did you stop beating your wife?" It can be used for nearly every interrogation:

"This is the first time you've ever cheated, isn't it, Bob?"
"You're sorry that you took the money, aren't you?"
"You're an honest person, and you'll never do it again, right?"
"You didn't molest any other children. Just this one time, correct?"

- **Give them time.** A good interrogation is like a good marinade, a tenderization of the meat. It takes time. Sometimes I'll leave a person in a room by himself to think about things for ten or twenty minutes, after which they usually give up the goods. Sometimes they beat themselves up in their own minds better than I ever could.

- **Lie.** Tell them you have evidence that shows that they committed whatever act they're denying. "We have you on video."

I was on a case in New Jersey where my client was missing a lot of jewelry and suspected several employees of theft. It was a big jewelry store. So I went there with a bunch of VHS tapes—this was the nineties—that were marked *Hidden Camera Five*, *Hidden Camera Six*, etc. Meanwhile, all those tapes had on them were recordings of *ALF* and *Who's the Boss?*

I started interviewing the employees. I said, "Listen, there are cameras you can see and there are cameras you can't throughout the store, and we have you on tape stealing this jewelry." It was a bluff. I didn't have anything. I interviewed fifteen people and was able to clear them all, just from their body language and what they were saying. However, there was this one little old lady who wouldn't come in to be interviewed. Nice old Jewish grandma. I said to her, "Why don't you come in?" She goes, "My sister died, and I'm still in mourning." Meanwhile, her sister died three months before, and she didn't even care for her sister. She was avoiding the issue.

I said, "Meet me at Dunkin' Donuts."

She did.

I said, "Listen, I have you on tape stealing jewelry, and we're going to take this to the prosecutor now and you're going to get arrested unless we can work this out."

"Okay," she said. "Can I talk to my lawyer?"

INTERROGATION
DO'S AND DON'TS

1. If you think your husband is cheating on you:
- Don't say: "You're banging the secretary, you lousy bum!"
- Do say:
  "What does she have that I don't?"
  "What can I do to make you happy?"
  "What can I do to make our marriage better?"

You will get the confession, and you can still throw him out in the end.

2. If you think your employee has stolen money from your firm:
- Don't say: "You're a thief and a liar."
  They'll clam up. They'll ask for their lawyer.
- Do say: "Things are hard these days. I remember stealing something once. You are not a bad guy. You made a mistake. Let's work this out. You will feel much better. I know I would."

Make them feel you are just like them. And when you get the confession, you can still fire them.

3. If you suspect your daughter is smoking marijuana:
- Don't say: "I *know* you're smoking dope. You better tell me."
- Do say: "Listen, honey, I'm concerned about you. Marijuana is bad for your health. You made a mistake. It's okay. Will you promise me that you're not going to do it again?"

Explain that you're trying to help them. Once they come clean, you can ground them for a year.

Now I know she's guilty. I said, "You want to talk to your lawyer? Then I'll let the prosecutor speak to your lawyer after you're arrested. You want to bring lawyers into this? I don't want to bring lawyers. I just want to settle this between you and me."

She said, "Okay. Can I talk to my husband? He's in the car."

She left, came back, and said, "I'll give you the stuff back."

I went to her house, and she gave me back more than what the owner even knew was missing!

THE POLYGRAPH

Much of my time as a private investigator is spent doing credibility assessment using a polygraph, more commonly called a lie detector test. Professional examiners use a polygraph to measure and record a person's physiological responses—blood pressure, pulse, respiration, and skin conductivity—while he or she answers a series of questions. There are three types of questions that are asked during a polygraph:

- **Irrelevant questions:** The answers for these you will already know. *Is your name Sam Smith?*

- **Profile questions:** You will already have a good idea what the answer will be. *Have you ever lied to get out of trouble?*

Taking a Polygraph

A WORD ABOUT HANDHELD LIE DETECTORS

There are gadgets on the market that are billed as handheld lie detectors—if you place them in the palm of someone's hand, they can measure everything from cardio and pulse to skin response to various stimuli. While these things are fun for parlor tricks and kids' birthday parties, they're a far cry from the sensitive polygraph equipment used by professionals. Polygraph testing is not a simple diagnostic test. It is a complex series of credibility assessment tests administered by a trained and experienced examiner. Chart interpretation is very analytical and numerically based. My advice? Save your money.

- **Relevant questions:** These are the answers you really want to know. *Did you kill Emma Miller on August 12, 2008?*

Deceptive answers will produce different physiological responses than non deceptive answers, and this allows the polygraph examiner to detect if a person is being truthful. However, there are certain misnomers regarding the use of polygraphs:

1. People only agree to take a polygraph if they're innocent. False. Although it seems counter intuitive, some people take a polygraph even though they know they are guilty. Why?

- Bravado. They figure they'll roll the dice, or if the results show they're guilty, they'll say, "I was nervous. I didn't do it. Your results are wrong."
- Deep down, they want to get found out. Very often, people

who are guilty will actually call *The Steve Wilkos Show* and say that they want to come on and take a polygraph, because, for example, their wife thinks they did something to their daughter. They usually wind up failing the test miserably. Subconsciously, they wanted to be exposed.

2. Refusing to submit to one is a sign of guilt.

False. There are many reasons why someone will not take a polygraph. Sometimes a subject's lawyer or union representative may have advised against it.

3. You can force someone to take a polygraph.

False. You cannot conduct a polygraph on someone who doesn't want to take it. However, an investigator hired by a parent or company owner, for example, can require a subject to take part in an *interview* as part of an investigation, particularly if theft or another crime has been committed.

4. The polygraph examiner will mistake my nervousness for guilt and get a *false positive*.

False. False positives for a polygraph—results that incorrectly indicate guilt—are minimized by modern testing techniques. Polygraphs are administered several times for accuracy and repeatability to make sure the examinee has the same reactions each time. There are also safeguards built into the scoring systems that create huge gaps between pass and fail. *Inconclusive* is a possible score if someone does not meet the scoring thresholds for *deception* or *no deception* indicated. However, a false positive is very rare.

5. A polygraph examiner will misread someone's facial tics as a sign of deception.

False. An experienced polygraph examiner will establish a baseline for all your leg bouncing, eye blinking, and other nervous tics in order to rule them out and focus on the more telling aspects of your body language.

6. It is possible to *beat* a polygraph.

False. It is not possible to beat a polygraph. However, you can beat the examiner.

What do I mean?

I am a very experienced polygraph examiner and am skilled at picking out countermeasures or techniques for hiding guilt, whether during a polygraph or a credibility assessment examination. Examiners who have recently come out of school are not. It's no different from comparing a medical student to a doctor who has practiced medicine for many years—if you go into a doctor's office complaining of certain symptoms, a young doctor just out of school may not be able to figure out what you've got, whereas a seasoned physician, who has seen it all, can probably give you a diagnosis on the spot.

The same goes for polygraphing. Newbies may not know what to look for or can misread test results, particularly if the person taking the test is skilled in performing what's called *intentional distortion* or mental countermeasures:

- Trying to alter breathing patterns during testing.
- Attempting to mentally block out test questions by doing complex equations backward in their heads—*two hundred minus seven is one hundred ninety three, minus seven is one hundred eighty six and so on*—so that they don't react.
- Trying to artificially increase their heart rate during polygraph testing by thinking of something scary or exciting or, possibly, by pricking themselves with a sharp object.

What these clowns don't realize is that doing this will create other physiological reactions and readings throughout the test that an experienced polygraph examiner will pick up on.

Obtaining information from a person who does not want to provide it takes great observation and great patience—it's like a championship boxing match with lots of rounds. Before the big match up, it is important that you have researched the facts of your case as well as your subject's background, and that, if possible, you have the documentation to back up your claims. Be ready to go the distance if you can't land the knockout punch in the early rounds. The truth really is out there. With enough preparation and practice, you'll be able to find it. ■

5

PROOF POSITIVE:
HOW TO GATHER
EVIDENCE

It's easy to accuse somebody of a crime or of wrongdoing. Nowadays, accusations fly left and right on the Internet and even on television news or tabloid programs where opinions, not facts, seem to be the order of the day. When it comes to investigating, however, the truth is this: you need to have evidence—*direct* evidence—to make an allegation or a claim stick.

WHAT IS EVIDENCE?

Evidence is information that supports a claim, suspicion, or theory. In a court of law, evidence is considered anything (documents, testimonies) that can prove *means, motive,* and *opportunity*:

- **Means:** Did the person own a gun or other

weapon with which he could have committed this crime?
Evidence: store receipt, gun license.

• **Motive:** Did he have something to gain? Revenge? An inheritance? A college admission? A raise or promotion? Evidence: a will or other bank documentation, witness testimony.

• **Opportunity:** Did he have a key to the liquor cabinet? Does he work nearby? Was he seen in the area?
Evidence: Key, security camera footage, smartphone photo.

The more evidence that you have, the better. A good private investigator will function like a journalist to find whatever evidence is out there, often using a series of fact-finding strategies:

1. Dig, dig, dig. Search online. Talk to witnesses. Visit locales.
2. Use reliable sources—credible, respectable, and objective suppliers of information. Web sites ending in .org are good ones.
3. Corroborate or confirm eyewitness accounts and testimonies, whenever and wherever possible.
4. Document—either by image or audio, or in writing.

That means that if you want to catch someone ripping you off or scamming you, you not only have to find and collect direct evidence of the crime, but you need to preserve the evidence so that it is convincing and, if need be, admissible.

Very often, I am hired as an investigator for the prosecutor or the defense attorney of a civil or criminal court case in order to gather evidence. Believe it or not, many attorneys are not very good at knowing what kinds of evidence are available and how to acquire them. Therefore, a lot of my work is evidentiary consulting— locating evidence legally and imaginatively, and handing it over to the attorneys, so that they can, in turn, present it in court.

There are various ways to gather information, depending on what is needed. As with finding missing persons, you have both offline and online resources at your disposal.

A WORD ABOUT
CIRCUMSTANTIAL
EVIDENCE

Not all evidence is created equal. *Direct* evidence supports a claim without the need for additional inquiry or information. *Circumstantial* evidence, on the other hand, relies on an inference to connect it to a conclusion of fact and may not be enough to prove a claim. For example, a fingerprint may place a suspect at the scene of a crime, but it does not give any indication as to what time the suspect was there. Other examples:

- You suspect your husband is cheating on you, and you find a cocktail napkin in the pocket of his suit jacket. Not enough evidence: He could have been having drinks with friends.
- Your teenage son told you that he was spending the weekend at a friend's house, but when you drove into town you saw his car parked in front of his girlfriend's house. Not enough evidence: There may be a reasonable explanation for this.
- You're in the middle of a child custody dispute, and your husband tells you he is employed, but you found an unemployment pay stub of his that's dated four weeks back. Not enough evidence: He may have found permanent employment since that date.

Circumstantial evidence doesn't tell you the whole story. What it does give you is the impetus to do further investigating. It can be the first piece of a very big puzzle.

GATHERING PHYSICAL EVIDENCE

Like conducting stakeouts, gathering physical evidence is probably what most people picture when they think of private investigation—guys holed up in a tenth-floor apartment snapping

TYPES OF PHYSICAL EVIDENCE

- Incriminating documentation
- Hair
- Fibers or threads
- Seminal stains
- Bloodstains
- Fingerprints
- Controlled substances

photos of suspicious-looking men in pinstriped suits through the window of a high rise across the street. There are all kinds of evidence that can be used to prove a claim. Are you ready? It's time to get down and dirty.

THE FINE ART OF GARBAGE RETRIEVAL

I told you it would get dirty. . . .

Sifting through someone's garbage can be a good way to find evidence of a crime or wrongdoing, particularly in the form of documentation, such as credit card statements, bank statements, check stubs, love letters, high school report cards, or E-ZPass statements. *What do you mean you weren't in Manhattan last month? Your statement has you driving through the Midtown Tunnel at 6:28 P.M. on May 28.* Sometimes you may find crucial household items or clothing, such as a semen-stained dress, if you suspect your wife is cheating.

Taking someone's trash is perfectly legal. Law enforcement does it all the time. In 1988, the Supreme Court ruled that once an item has been left for garbage pickup, there is no expectation of privacy or continued ownership—that goes for items discarded at the side of your house or in your office wastepaper basket (making them fair game for cleanup crews).

However, you can't conduct garbage retrieval if the garbage is on private property, unless you have been given permission to be there (as with cleanup crews). In other words, the Supreme Court says that although you have abandoned the property, I cannot go onto your property to retrieve it. Technically, you still have custody of that property. Therefore, trash retrieval from an outdoor can—commonly known as *Dumpster diving*—cannot be conducted if that can is located in a backyard or at the side of a house.

So what do you do if you want access to someone's garbage, but it's located in a can that's on private property? You wait for the garbage collection days. Once the cans are moved to the curb, which is considered public property, you can take what you need.

However, I've had some cases where the sanitation department collected the garbage straight from the sides of people's houses, not the curbs. What did I do then?

I paid off the garbage collector to give me what I needed. I waited down the street, and when the truck came down the block,

GARBAGE RETRIEVAL CHECKLIST

Mask: To protect your eyes.

Gloves: To protect your hands from cuts, burns, germs, etc.

Wipes/Disinfectant: You need cleaning supplies of some kind to clean the trash—or clean you—because along with the documents you need you're going to find chicken bones, peas, etc. We did an investigation on one of the largest armored truck losses in United States history, and the family we were watching had kids in diapers. It was not pleasant picking through their garbage!

Patience: If the documents you're looking for have been strip-cut shredded—cut into narrow strips that are as long as the original sheet of paper—you'll be at it for a while, laying the strips out and piecing them together, one by one, like a puzzle. (If the paperwork is crosscut shredded—it has been cut into rectangular, parallelogram, or diamond-shaped shreds—you're pretty much out of luck.) It can be done. I've made multimillion-dollar fraud cases out of garbage. One man's trash is another man's treasure.

I flagged one of the workers and said, "Dude, I'm going to give you a hundred dollars a week for that house's garbage. When you collect it, don't throw it in the back of the truck. Hold on to it, and I'll meet you at the end of the block each pick-up day at seven o'clock in the morning, and we'll make the exchange." Technically, the garbage collector was taking the trash legally—the resident had given the garbage collector permission to come and take it. I was just exploiting an opening.

INFORMANTS

In Chapter 3, we discussed using informants as a way to find people. We can also use them as a way to find *information* about people: What time do they leave their house every morning to go to work? What kinds of deliveries do they get (food, flowers, furniture)? Where do they eat out most? You'd be surprised how much information people pick up about others without realizing it.

However, most people generally don't want to get involved in other people's business or litigation, so if I approach them as the hired private investigator on behalf of an attorney, they tend to clam up. Therefore, as with other areas of private investigation, I have to perform subterfuge—pose as a freelance writer, an employer, an old boyfriend—to get them to talk. If I can do that

TIPS FOR USING INFORMANTS

- Look professional and polished, not creepy.
- Be prepared to answer any question that the informant might have with confidence and assurance.
- Be courteous.
- Offer an incentive, usually cash.

If you play your cards right, you can find out a person's underwear size. You really can.

and document the information I receive (remember to review state privacy laws regarding the recording of video and audio, as discussed in Chapter 2), I can get everything I need. (Occasionally, I may need the informant to testify at a trial or hearing. If I do, I will go back to that person, apologize for lying, admit to being an investigator, and ask him to appear in court. Although the informant may be ticked off, at that point he has to appear voluntarily, since I already have his statement, or else the attorney will issue a subpoena requiring him to do so.)

OPENING DOORS

Doormen are some of the best informants I've had. They know *everything* about the comings and goings of their apartment buildings—who's banging whom, who's on vacation, who keeps ordering stuff from the blow-up doll company. They're indispensible.

In the early nineties, I was on a litigation case for a pharmaceutical company, which was started by an older gentleman who took in a young chemist as his partner. There was a thirty-year age difference between the two of them, but the pair worked together for many years, and when the older gentleman retired, the younger partner bought the older gentleman's company shares for about two million dollars. Years later, the older gentleman's sister, who had nothing to do with him for many years, accused the young chemist of scamming her brother—who had since developed dementia—out of money that belonged to her, since she was the next of kin. I was hired by the chemist's attorney to prove that at the time the deal was made the older gentleman was lucid.

How was I going to do that?

I went to the old man's Manhattan apartment building, where he had lived for about a hundred years, and told the doorman I was writing an article on the guy, who was now eighty-five years old and had been a pioneer in the pharmaceutical industry. The only information I had was that the guy had prostate surgery on a certain date, after which he had a stroke, and that the deal had been signed before the surgery. But when did he develop dementia? Was it after the stroke or sometime before?

I said to the doorman, "I understand he had prostate surgery and then he had a stroke and wasn't the same."

"Oh, yeah," the doorman said. "Different guy."

"Before the prostate surgery," I asked, "how was he?"

"Oh, he was unbelievable. He would come down and play the violin for us. He would do one-armed pushups." Because the old guy never got married and never had kids, he had no real friends or family, so he would hang out with the doormen.

"Would you talk with him?" I asked. "Have discussions?"

"Sure, he would talk about politics and about what was going on in the world. I never realized he was so smart. He was sharper than a twenty year old."

Bingo!

"Do you mind if I record you, so that I don't have to take notes?" I asked.

"No problem."

"Who were his friends?" I asked.

"Oh, George from the diner." He told me the old guy ate at the corner diner for breakfast, lunch, and dinner every day.

I went to see George, who told me, "Every day, we talked about politics, the world. He'd play the violin."

That was it. I busted the case wide open in an hour, all from asking myself: *How can I get information from these people?* If, instead, I had said to the doorman, "There's a lawsuit going on, and I want you to be a witness," I wouldn't have gotten anything. You need to make your questioning inert, show them that it's not going to hurt them. People are concerned primarily about themselves.

Another time, I had to conduct a surveillance on a woman who worked in a large building on the Upper West Side of Manhattan. I didn't know who she was. All the information I had was that she was a psychologist who fit the average description—mid forties, brown hair, glasses—and the address of the apartment building where she lived. How the hell was I going to pick her out?

TAKING A STATEMENT

It is imperative that you record an informant's or witness's statement in some way. You should do this for your own protection:

- You don't want to make a mistake and jot the wrong information down. Even if you are an expert typist and bring a laptop along, there is still room for error.
- You will be covered in case informants or witnesses decide to change their minds, or if they blame you for leading them in a certain direction or for coercion.

For audio or video recordings (check state privacy laws), be sure to have the witness:

- State the date, time, day, and place, and that he or she agrees to the recording.
- State his or her full name, address, and phone number.
- State her occupation and place of employment (if necessary).
- Speak in a controlled and clear voice.

For written statements:

- Have the witness write the document him- or herself.
- Have the witness initial each page, and sign and date the document's last page.
- Make a copy, and send it to the witness as a sign of goodwill (you may need him again), but always keep the original in a safe place.

Enter the doorman.

"Listen," I said, approaching the guy, "you want to make fifty dollars?"

"Yeah," the guy said.

I told him the woman's name. "Do you know her?"

"Yeah," he said again. Talkative guy.

"Okay, I'm going to stand across the street near my car. When she comes out, just point to her."

The doorman said, "Okay, no problem." Then he added, "You're not going to hurt her, are you?"

I said, "No. No. We're just conducting an investigation. She was in an accident." I made something up on the spot.

Of course, you run the risk of the informant telling the target about your offer, so you've got to gauge how money-hungry he is before you give up what's going on. It's usually best to give a pretext—you have to serve her with a subpoena to appear in court, she's a witness to an incident with a patient, whatever it might be. Ideally, try not to give out the real reason you want her identified, so there's no chance of anyone squealing.

The guy said, "No problem."

I told him to be discreet, but when the woman came out of the building, the doorman looked like he was having a convulsion—pointing and pantomiming. He gave her right up. For money, they'll sell you their mothers.

ALL IN THE FAMILY

In addition to doormen and other service workers—delivery guys and porters—some of the best informants have turned out to be family members, especially if there's been a falling out of some kind between them and your target.

I had a recent case involving a stalker where the guy had mental issues and was writing letters to a CEO of a very big company. I was doing a threat assessment, which involves finding out what level of risk the person possesses to my client. Does he have access to weapons? Does he have a criminal history? Has he been violent before? Along those lines. I really couldn't find much on this guy, but I found his brother through a public record search. I called up his brother, who told me, "I haven't spoken to my brother in years, but my brother's freaking crazy."

Perfect. The brother seemed ready to talk. In my research, I noticed that the brother was a musician, so I assumed he was some starving-artist type with long hair.

I said, "Listen, do you want to make five hundred dollars?"

The guy said, "Yeah."

I said, "Give me your brother's biography, his history."

He said, "My brother grew up here, and then he moved in with my father, because my parents have been divorced since I was four. My mother sent him to live with my dad because he was a problem kid." He told me the name of the high school his brother went to.

"Did he graduate?" I asked.

"Yes."

"What sports did he play?"

"He was involved in wrestling."

"Was he violent?" (You like how I slipped that in there?)

"He's never been violent."

I said, "I never found an arrest record."

"He's never been arrested."

I said, "So what's your brother's problem? Why does he act this way?"

He said, "It's the drugs. He's done meth for many, many years."

"Yeah, but your brother drives a nice car."

"My brother is a really good scam artist. He can make you believe certain things, and he gets jobs, and he gets money. Then he doesn't perform, and he gets fired."

WHEN IS A JOB TOO BIG FOR AN AMATEUR?

If it's a criminal investigation or if there might be legal ramifications, leave it to the professionals. For serious matters, you don't want to tamper with evidence or ruin your chances of being a credible witness, especially in your own case. That's why you hire private investigators—they're professional and neutral.

"How does he normally live?"

"Honestly, I think he does male prostitution, but I'm not sure."

I was able to find out that the subject had no history of violence and no access to guns, he wasn't into hunting, weapons, or archery, and, as far as the brother knew, he hadn't ever hurt anyone. And I got it all straight from the horse's brother's mouth.

I wrote a report to my client, who said to me, "How the hell did you get all this information?" It made me look like a champ, and it made the brother five hundred bucks. Think about it: Wouldn't your brother know all the things you've done?

Again, there could have been consequences. Would the informant tell his brother? Is he telling me the truth? You have to get a feel for the informant and think about his motivations. Investigation is like a game of chess—think carefully about whatever piece you move. You may need to give up a few pawns to get the king.

HOWDY, NEIGHBOR!

Who better to get information from than a target's neighbor or coworker? The people I work with and live near probably know more about what's going on in my life than my closest friends! However, with these types of informants, you really run the risk of them tattling on you, especially if they're close friends with the person you're trying to investigate. That's why it's important to utilize a pretext. These have worked for me in the past:

- Your neighbor/coworker has applied for some credit. *Can you please tell me about him?*
- Your neighbor/coworker is applying for a job. *We can't really tell you what it is, since it's confidential, but what kind of neighbor/ coworker is he?*
- Your neighbor/coworker wants to be a soccer coach (if you know he has little kids). *What can you tell us?*
- We're writing a newspaper article about your neighbor/coworker who is getting an award. *Shhh . . . it's a surprise. Can you tell us a little about him?*

From a brief conversation with a neighbor or coworker, you'll get a good feel for a person. "He's a good guy." "He's a creepy guy." "He killed my cat." Whatever it might be.

One time, I was doing a threat assessment on a guy who was mailing some disturbing letters to a celebrity client of mine. I knew where the guy lived from the return address on the letters—some of these people really aren't that bright—so I knocked on his neighbor's door. The pretext was that I wanted to move into the neighborhood and was wondering if he could tell me about the schools and the community members. I asked about his immediate neighbors, and he told me the guy we were looking at lived at home, was slightly disabled, read the Bible, and had a wife and a bicycle (no car). Turned out, he was a little crazy, but basically harmless. I then spoke to the actual subject and took several photos of him secretly with my smartphone.

I deemed him a low risk. He was unemployed, slightly delusional, and a religious fanatic. He had no easy way to travel hundreds of miles to get to my client, and no criminal history. We wound up simply calling him up on the phone and telling him to knock it off. I gave the photos of the guy to my client, so he would know what he looked like and could give the photos to his doorman, his security people at the TV studio, etc., in case the guy ever showed up.

Sometimes neighbors will do more than give you information. We've used neighbors' property to conduct a surveillance when we've needed to watch a home for an extended period of time. On a recent case, I went to a neighbor across the street from my target and said, "Can I pay you fifty dollars a day to set up a camera to watch your neighbor?" The guy said, "Yeah. I hate that guy. No problem."

I had another case in Florida where the woman I was watching was faking a back and neck injury in order to collect millions of dollars from her insurance company. She would show up at her depositions in a neck brace and lie on the floor to give testimony! She was very, very surveillance conscious—she had the neighborhood kids ride around on their bicycles looking for strange cars. She lived on a block where the residents didn't park on the street, so any car parked there was going to set her off. We had to outfox her.

One of her neighbors was painting his garage. We approached him and said, "Listen, we're investigators. We're watching somebody, but we can't sit on the street. Can we pay you fifty dollars a day to park on your driveway?" He said, "Yeah, that'll pay for the paint for my house." So we're sitting on the guy's driveway, and the woman comes out of her house. She's looking and looking around the street, and nobody's there. When she sees the coast is clear, she starts gardening, she starts chasing the dog around her front yard. Meanwhile, we're there filming her. At some point, no matter how careful they are, everybody makes a mistake. It's just a matter of you, as an investigator, catching them and documenting it.

DRUG TESTING

A drug test is the technical analysis of a biological specimen of a person—for example, urine, blood, or other fluids—to determine the presence of a specified drug. As an employer, you may have the right to ask your employee to submit to a drug test, although I always suggest consulting with a qualified employment attorney before asking any employee to participate in drug or DNA testing. (Laws vary from state to state as to what is permissible for an employer to request from an employee.)

Recently, I got a call from a doctor—a Park Avenue surgeon—who had a lot of cash and checks missing. Turned out, it was her office manager, a very pretty Italian girl who lived in an affluent New York suburb. The girl was basically robbing her blind. Why? She had an Oxycodone addiction, and the surgeon never drug-tested her before hiring her. All she had to do was go to the local drugstore—drug test kits are also available online—and buy a simple drug test for twenty-five dollars, hand it to her employee, and say, "Go make pee-pee."

FINGERPRINT ANALYSIS

A fingerprint remains unchanged throughout a person's lifetime, and until DNA testing came along, it was the primary way of

BASIC FINGERPRINT PATTERNS

- Loop patterns
  (65 percent of all fingerprints):
  Ridges flow in one side, recurve
  (or loop around), pass through
  an imaginary line drawn from
  the delta to the core, and exit
  the pattern on the same side
  from which it entered.

- Whorl patterns
  (30 percent of all fingerprints):
  A series of almost concentric
  circles.

- Arch patterns
  (5 percent of all fingerprints):
  Ridges flow in one side and
  out the opposite side. There
  are no deltas.

identifying individuals. Investigators continue to use fingerprint analysis, particularly if there is an absence of DNA, for a variety of reasons, including background checks, theft, or identifying amnesia victims or deceased John or Jane Does.

Fingerprints are classified into three categories, each of which comes with a specific way of collecting them:

- **Patent:** These fingerprints are often found in blood, oil, or ink, or on surfaces such as glass. They are easily spotted and can be photographed with any camera that captures high resolution images.

- **Impressed:** These prints are made in soft material or tissue by pressing down with the finger or hand. They also can be photographed (or sometimes professionals will make molds of them if they are very fragile).

ANATOMY OF A
FINGERPRINT

- Bifurcation: A ridge divides into two ridges, like a fork in the road.
- Core: In a loop fingerprint, this is the center of the loop.
- Crossover: Ridges appear to cross over each other.
- Delta: Ridges meet from three directions. (There is usually one delta on a loop and two or more on a whorl.)
- Island: Short ridges cut off from others.
- Ridge end: An individual ridge comes to an end.

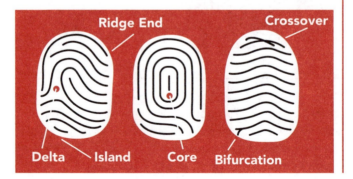

- **Latent:** These prints are not visible to the naked eye. Your fingers have tiny pores that release sweat, and those pores also pick up salts, oils, and tiny particles of dirt, which are what make up latent prints. These prints can only been seen with the use of ultraviolet lights, magnesium powders, or other chemical agents. You can purchase these items online or through law enforcement supply stores. The magnesium powders come in a variety of colors, such as cash box gray and manila folder yellow. This way, if you are a business owner and suspect one of your employees is rifling through your cash box or file cabinet, you can use a tiny paintbrush to apply a layer of gray or yellow powder to the box or cabinet. When the culprit touches the box or files, the powder, which is invisible to the naked eye, will transfer to his hands. It will stick to him even if he washes his hands, and it will transfer to whatever is in his hand—a pen, his cell phone, his car keys. The next morning, you can ask your employees to show you their hands and shine a black light over them—the guilty hands will fluoresce. These powders, in their assortment of colors, can be dusted onto anything from money and doorknobs to confidential files, cookie jars, and liquor cabinets. Although security cameras have mostly replaced the use of these powders, they are still a good option, because they are much cheaper and easier to install.

DNA TESTING

DNA is a powerful tool for identification. Unlike fingerprints, which rely on a subject touching an object, DNA exists in every cell of the human body—from hair to blood to skin—all of which can be shed. DNA databases have millions of records, and law enforcement laboratories can electronically search and compare DNA profiles to collect evidence.

Today, you can purchase DNA test kits from selected drugstores and also online from websites such as the DNA Diagnostics Center (dnacenter.com), which has certified facilities around the country where samples can be collected; you can also mail in samples depending upon what is being tested. There are many applications beyond forensic testing in a criminal investigation for which you would use DNA. These include:

- **Determining paternity.** To find out if a child is biologically yours.

- **Determining familial relationships.** Often, siblings are split up into different foster homes, or maybe you are in search of your birth mother. You can take a DNA test to see if you and others share certain DNA.

- **Proving infidelity.** For this claim, a DNA test is usually conducted following a semen test, which determines the presence of semen. (This too can be purchased online.) If the material tests positive for semen, it's now a matter of determining to whom it belongs, and for that you can conduct a DNA test. Keep in mind that this is an expensive process. A DNA extract from a stain and comparison to a sample can cost thousands of dollars!

- **Dealing with workplace matters.** Recently, I was hired by a secretary who was concerned about a letter she had received that she believed came from this creepy guy working in her office. I said, "Don't handle the letter. Let's look to see if there's contact DNA." We took it, sent it out, and got a positive DNA sample off the saliva where the envelope had been licked. Then we asked the creepy employee-guy if he would willingly give us a DNA sample. He said he didn't write this letter and volunteered his DNA. It didn't match, so we cleared him.

GATHERING EVIDENCE ONLINE

Many of the online resources we use to gather information about people are the same ones we use to find them, as we discussed in Chapter 3. These include:

- **Search engines:** Has your subject been in the news?

HOW **TO ACQUIRE** DNA

1. Get permission, if necessary. Tests for paternity, for example, require a subject to sign a consent form (if he doesn't agree, you can only conduct a paternity test by court order); however, most DNA kits require only the signature of a responsible adult—that's *you*—for reading and accepting the terms and conditions. In other words, no permission is needed for DNA tests conducted for peace of mind.

2. Obtain a specimen. Always follow the kit directions, which will probably include the use of gloves and disposable instruments, such as cotton swabs, and avoid touching areas where DNA evidence could exist. A good specimen requires only a few cells of any of the following:
   - Blood
   - Semen
   - Skin
   - Saliva
   - Hair
   - Fingernails/toenails
   - Mucus
   - Sweat
   - Earwax

3. Cross-contamination is always an issue with specimens, so take great care when collecting DNA. Try to refrain from talking, sneezing, or coughing over the evidence or from touching your face and then touching an area that may contain the DNA to be tested.

- **Professional or company Web sites:** Is he the majority shareholder in a firm?

- **Public records Web sites:** How many properties does he own?

- **Social media:** Was he in the Bahamas last Christmas?

- Set up a Google Alert (google .com/alerts) for a subject's name or alias in order to get notifications from Google when his or her name pops up somewhere online.
- Use your browser's search function to locate your subject's name within a Web site.

- **Virtual globe, map, and geographical information programs (Google Earth):** Does he own a swimming pool?

Using a combination of these resources, you can assemble a profile: Does this guy have money? Can I sue him and collect? What kind of neighborhood does he live in? What's the average value of the homes? You'll be able to locate assets, conduct preliminary background checks and screenings, and get a better idea of the kind of person you're dealing with. All for free.

GLOSSARY

Due diligence: a fancy word for background investigation
Run a DMV: perform a Department of Motor Vehicles check for either a driver's license or vehicle registration.
VIN: Vehicle Identification Number

HOW TO LOCATE ASSETS

Assets come in different forms—businesses, homes, cars. Most people's biggest asset is their house, and real property is very easy to find online (as discussed in Chapter 3) because it's public record, and you can get a good idea of people's net worth.

For example, if you get a judgment against someone and want to collect on that judgment, you can conduct a property search and discover that person owns a big house in upstate New York. You can then place a lien on that person's house, which essentially means he cannot sell that house until he pays the money he owes you. (A title search company will see there's a lien on the house and will not transfer the title.)

PUBLIC
RECORDS THAT SHOW
ASSETS

Division of Corporations: Most states have their own divisions and/or Web sites. All you have to do is type in the person's name to conduct an entity search.

Department of Assessment: The Department of Assessment collects and records relevant residential, commercial, and industrial property information, usually by county.

ACRIS: In New York City, you can use the Automated City Register Information System, as detailed in Chapter 3, to view any property that has a deed, mortgage, or lien attached to it. Other municipalities have similar systems that can tell you how much a subject paid for a property, how much the previous owners paid for it, the number of units, the square footage, the tax value, etc. You can also view those properties on a map.

Department of Motor Vehicles (DMV): It's a little more difficult to look at Department of Motor Vehicles records because some states have DMV privacy laws. However, you can contact the DMV in your state and tell the contact there that you are looking for assets for a judgment, and see if he or she can help you.

Company Web sites: If your subject is the major shareholder in a public technology company, you can get a pretty good financial picture of that person (privately held companies do not release this kind of information). At the very least, there may be computers that you can seize.

Social media sites: You might win a judgment against a guy, who tells you he's broke and can't pay up. A little social media research might turn up a photo of him and a young blonde on a boat with the caption: *Spending the day on my boat with my baby.* Then it's anchors aweigh for you!

P.I. GLOSSARY

Hidden assets: anything of value that you want to conceal or protect, including items that are not registered, such as cash or jewelry, as well as those that are, including real property, businesses, or bank accounts. Once, I was working a matrimonial case for a wife whose husband was an investment banker, and he told the court that all he had was thirty thousand dollars. I ended up finding twelve million dollars that he was hiding in Vanuatu, an island near Fiji. (They had a season of *Survivor* there.) When the wife's attorney went to court and told the judge, "Your honor, we found twelve million dollars," the husband literally passed out. They had to call the EMTs and get him to the hospital!

If no property comes up, you may find through the Department of Motor Vehicles that the person has a classic Corvette or a Harley Davidson motorcycle that has been paid off. You can give that information to the local sheriff or marshal, so that he can go and seize them. Law enforcement will come with a tow truck, take his property, and give it to you in satisfaction of the judgment. (Keep in mind that the marshal and the sheriff are not going to do the asset searches for you. You have to do them yourself and say, "Here are the assets. Go get them." Or you have to engage an investigator to find and retrieve the assets.)

BACKGROUND CHECKS

A background check is the process of compiling criminal, commercial, and financial records of an individual or organization. Conducting one is done the same way you would go about finding a person, missing or otherwise: by utilizing public records, such as court or criminal records, to check for litigations, judgments, liens, bankruptcies, or crimes committed.

It's very important to know the truth about people, no matter how they appear or how many others referred them to you. Back in my jewelry manufacturing days, we used polishers who had worked with very prestigious firms, such as Tiffany & Co. Meanwhile, they were scammers and would keep the dust from the gold that they polished. (Raw gold is malleable, and, as it is polished, loses tiny pieces that, when collected, can add up to hundreds of thousands of dollars a year!) They used a vacuum system, and by the time they were done, I was missing forty thousand dollars in gold! I started running background checks on these guys and discovered they had a criminal history. You'd think working for Tiffany would have meant they had clean credentials. Obviously not. That's why you've always got to do your own homework.

Other reasons to conduct a background check:

- **Business ventures.** You may not want to take on a business partner who has had a string of business failures.

- **New tenants.** A new tenant just moved into your building, and you want to know if he has been in prison or was ever charged with a crime.

- **Pre-employment.** Good people can be hard to find.

One time, a cardiologist called me up. He had hired a Russian girl—a beautiful, petite, twenty-five-year-old blonde—for his practice in Brooklyn. Out of the blue, she started coming on to him. Keep in mind that he was a big, fat, ugly guy in his sixties—*not that there's anything wrong with that.* Anyway, she started coming on to him, and they started having consensual sex. She started giving him oral sex. He was having the time of his life! Meanwhile, unbeknownst to him, she had done this to other doctors, and she sued them all for sexual harassment. Sure enough, after a month or two of this sneaking around, the girl secretly set up a Web cam in his office. One day, she walked in, closed the door, and stood there looking at him. The cardiologist, who had become accustomed to the girl immediately jumping his bones, said, "Come here. Come over here. Come give me oral sex."

The girl said, "No. No. Leave me alone."

He said, "What do you mean *no?* Come on. Let's go."

The girl took the digital recording to a lawyer, and it looked like the cardiologist was trying to sexually attack her.

Now, common sense should have kicked in at some point. I mean, I'm all for May-December romances, but if the doctor had checked his ego at the door, he would have been suspicious the first time the girl made a sexual advance. And if he had conducted a background check, he would have discovered that she had been in similar litigation before, and he wouldn't have hired her. But he was too cheap, or too stupid, to hire an investigator to conduct the litigation search, which any private individual should have done to protect himself.

- **Dating.** Dating ain't what it used to be. Once upon a time you went on a first date only after you already met the person—unless it was a blind date, and even then it was usually set up by someone you knew and trusted. These days, with online dating, all you know about a person is what you read online, all of which can be fabricated. The person could be an ax murderer. Or a drug addict.

A few years back, a very wealthy woman called me up six months after I had worked on her divorce. She was a blonde, pretty woman in her fifties who lived in a beautiful house in a gated community on Long Island. Her name was Barbara, like my wife.

"Barb, hey, what's going on?" I asked.

"I met this guy," she said. "He looks like Fabio—blond, long hair, muscles. He plays the guitar. I met him at a bar. Three days later, he moved into my house. We make love every day. We walk, we hike with the dogs, he sings to me. He's just everything that I've ever imagined and dreamed of."

"Wow, sounds great," I said. "What's the matter?"

"My fifty-thousand-dollar diamond ring is missing," she said. *Wham.*

"What do you know about him?" I asked, and she told me his name and where he was from. "Does he have a car?"

"Yeah, he has this old Saab. He keeps it locked, and everything he has is in there."

I said, "Give me his license plate."

I ran the plate, and the vehicle registration matched the guy, so I had his date of birth. I ran his criminal record, and my printer almost exploded! It didn't stop printing. Pages and pages and pages:

Burglary
Burglary

DID YOU KNOW?

Bad guys and gals who have criminal histories move around a lot and change their names (women will use maiden names). Unless you run a nationwide background check and/or search, as opposed to only a state search, they can slip through the cracks. A New York jewelry store owner once contacted me to conduct a background check on a girl who applied for a position. I ran a check on her in New York State, and nothing came up. The owner mentioned that she also lived in Florida for a time, so I ran a check on her in Florida, and there was an open case for theft at a jewelry store where she had been working.

Burglary
Escaping from prison
Burglary
Burglary
Recently released from prison

The guy was a predicate felon. He had spent practically his whole life in prison—that was where he learned how to play the guitar and got those jailhouse muscles! And that's why he was so horny! And now he had found a nice blonde, and was driving her Lexus convertible, not working, and living rent-free. Luckily, the guy was an idiot and couldn't keep his sticky fingers to himself.

I sent a couple of retired cops over there to throw him out. They arrived with the guy's arrest record and said, "Don't ever come back here!"

The next day, Barbara called me up and said, "But I miss him."

I said, "Don't you start!"

One simple background check would have nipped this false romance in the bud, and I have many other similar cases. Scammers and scoundrels are everywhere!

Keep in mind that background checks only work if you're dealing with a bad guy with a history. A person could have committed a hundred crimes and never been caught, so a background check would turn up nothing, because he has no criminal record. Bernie Madoff—boy, did he have some resumé! He was the biggest scammer in the world, and he was the chairman of NASDAQ. Who the hell wouldn't trust the chairman of NASDAQ? A con man is a confidence man. He gains your confidence before he burns you. Unfortunately, there's really no way of knowing if you'll be someone's first victim, so it's best to rely on the tips we discussed in Chapter 4 on discerning deception, or to always listen to that human intuition to tell you that something isn't right. Don't be afraid to ask questions! The more you know, the better off you'll be. ■

6

OUT OF SITE: HOW TO VIRTUALLY DISAPPEAR

I know what you're thinking. . . .

How can there be a chapter titled How to Virtually Disappear when I just got through telling you in Chapter 3 that there's no way to go entirely off-grid because we all leave trails?

Good question.

And you're right. Somewhere along the line there is a record of you. For starters, nearly everyone in the United States has a birth certificate. (Even if you changed your name legally very early on, there will still be a record of that name change.) And from there, the evidence accrues—school records, voting records, etc. Heck, you can't even walk around a major city without your image being picked up by a street or security camera's face-recognition software. As I said in Chapter 3, the more accomplished or active you are as a U.S. citizen, and the more information you willingly divulge, particularly online, the easier it is to find you.

However, keep in mind that the reason we're all so easy to locate is that we don't really think about hiding or the imprints we leave—we spend our lives happily applying for credit cards, taking selfies, and detailing the daily escapades of our children and our pets on social media. We've become used to living our lives in the public eye for all to see, and don't consider the dangers of our exposure until something happens—our identity is stolen, some creep starts pestering us on Facebook, or there's a black sedan that's always parked outside our apartment. Then we feel naked and vulnerable and want to beef up our privacy precautions.

It's always a good exercise to take a step back and think about the kinds of information we put out there, whether it's once in a lifetime (once is often enough) or every day. The Internet has created a world of Peeping Toms, from harmless to criminal, who would like nothing better than to mess with you, find you, or take what's yours, so it's important to consider the decisions you make—or don't realize you make—about what they can and cannot see.

There are varying levels of public profile reduction:

- **Level 1:** Keeping average folks—from everyday yahoos and giggly fangirls to old classmates and money-grubbing relatives—from being able to find you. This level is probably where most people fall. They just want to be safe. And there are things you can do to limit your exposure and make it difficult for nosy but otherwise normal people to find you.

- **Level 2:** Keeping average—but persistent—folks from being able to find you. These people keep trying. Obsessed fans. Infatuated husbands or ex-boyfriends. Stalkers. Amateur private eyes. (We'll talk more about personal protection in Chapter 9.) For this group, you need to implement an extra layer of caution.

- **Level 3:** Keeping professional folks—repo men, bail bondsmen, bounty hunters, private investigators like me—from being able

REASONS
TO REDUCE PUBLIC
EXPOSURE

- You're a celebrity. The last thing you want are cameras following you to the local gym and snapping photos of you on the stair stepper. How you get those six-pack abs should be your little secret.
- You've been a victim of a crime such as domestic abuse, harassment, or stalking. Maybe your boyfriend won't leave you alone and keeps calling your cell phone, or you don't want your ex-wife to find you. (You should know that there are legal entities and organizations that can help you. For example, if you are the victim of domestic abuse, you can contact the National Domestic Violence Hotline at 1-800-799-7233 or thehotline.org.)
- You've been a victim of identity theft (we'll talk more about this in Chapter 8 with regard to how to have a more secure online presence rather than drop out of the public eye altogether).
- You are applying to college and want to present a professional and studious appearance. A photo of you passed out on a toilet bowl probably won't bode well for your chances of getting into Harvard.
- You have a specific privacy concern, such as those related to custody or marital matters.
- You want to monitor your children's public profiles to make sure they aren't unintentionally giving out too much information about themselves.
- You're a scammer and you've just run off with a boatload of cash, and now you don't want to be found. (But I *will* find you!)
- You're in the witness protection program.

to find you. This level is usually reserved for people who are on the run; maybe they've committed a crime, or are about to, have reneged on debts, or skipped bail. Professionals have access to resources that everyday sleuths do not, so you've got to practically disappear online and leave a virtual dead end for us professionals not to find you. (If you can escape my watchful eye, you're good. Otherwise, I'll track you down like a bloodhound.)

- **Level 4:** This level is for people who just have had it with mankind and want to ride off into the sunset alone (make sure you pay cash for your horse). This keeps anyone and everyone—friends and family included—from being able to find you. Basically, you'll be living on a deserted island somewhere combing beaches, cracking open coconuts, and conversing with your only friend: a volleyball named Wilson. This is doable, but, as you'll read, you have to be willing to give up a lot for this kind of seclusion.

LEVEL 1: KEEPING THE HARMLESS—BUT ANNOYING— FOLKS AWAY

The average stalker has a quick attention span. He or she will probably search for you over the course of a few days or a month, lose interest when there's nothing readily available, and move on to something—or someone—else. Fans usually fall into this category. (There are only so many cards and letters you can write to Justin Bieber before you realize that the kid is probably not going to marry you.) In order to keep these people at bay, you don't need to withdraw completely from your online practices. You just may need to modify them.

- **Web sites.** On any Web-sites you own and operate, don't list an address or a telephone number. You want to keep from popping up in a quick White Pages search. If you must have a mailing address available, maybe for work purposes, it's best to use a PO box, preferably in another town, if you don't mind the drive.

- **E-mail address.** Don't use your personal e-mail address. You usually receive more than one e-mail address when setting up a domain and Web site. Have public correspondence filter to one that's separate from your personal communications, so that you can always shut one down and use another if you get too many pests or haters.

- **Third parties.** Use some kind of buffer: an agent, a publicist, your brother Joe. Rather than deal directly with cold callers or prospective clients, have them go through an intermediary who will pass on any bona fide prospects. This goes for both e-mails and phone calls. This way, you can still keep the lines of communication open, but keep them from funneling directly to you.

- **Social media.** Heighten social media privacy settings. Most social networking Web sites allow you to block friends or followers, to report suspicious behavior to the Web sites's head honchos, or to turn public accounts into private accounts. Make use of those settings.

- **Building security.** Give doormen a list of all acceptable visitors, or advise them to handle all unannounced visitors.

- **Phones.** Don't answer blocked calls, private number calls, or calls from numbers you don't know. Let those calls go to voice mail so you can screen them.

LEVEL 2: KEEPING THE PERSISTENT—AND WORRISOME—FOLKS AWAY

You know when an interaction turns sour. That really nice guy you met at the bar with whom you swapped business cards suddenly is calling at all hours of the night. A casual e-mail correspondence with a colleague suddenly turns too personal. You start getting hate mail from strangers, because of a political blog post you wrote. When harmless interactions turn into worrisome events, it's time to really batten down the hatches and

P.I. GLOSSARY

Mail drop: utilizing a mail-receiving service, such as a UPS Store or Mailboxes Etc., rather than a physical address so that you can receive your mail in anonymity. I used one for many years when I was working out of my house and didn't want to use my home address. One day, the guy at the UPS Store called me to tell me two guys had come in looking for me.

keep all public communications to a minimum. What additional precautions should you take?

- **Web sites.** You should take down all contact points on Web sites. These include contact forms, e-mail addresses, mailing addresses, and phone numbers.

- **Social media.** You can choose to do away with your social media altogether or adjust your privacy settings to the strictest ones available, which will, depending upon the site, keep people from being able to see, follow, or message you.

- **Building security.** Advise doormen of particular people who are not welcome if they should come calling for you.

- **Phones.** Block texts and calls on your smartphone from any particular people to whom you do not wish to speak.

- **Get help.** Make a police report if threatened or stalked.

LEVEL 3: VIRTUALLY DISAPPEARING

Okay, now things get tricky. Laying low is one thing, but trying to virtually erase an online presence can be difficult. You're already on the grid—unless you've been planning your disappearance for years and have been shedding your public persona piece by piece—and there's really nothing you can do to erase your digital footprint thus far. If, today, you decide that you want to hide or go off-grid, there's a lot that you need to do. First, you need to have a plan:

- Make sure you have enough cash to get you where you want to go and sustain you.
- You'll have to throw your friends and loved ones off your track, since if anyone knows where you are it increases your chances of being found. You can:
    - Create false entries in a diary.
    - Leave a note that throws people off track.

- Book trips on flights that you have no intention of taking.
- Tell everyone you know how excited you are about moving somewhere, and then move somewhere else. When my uncle relocated to Israel several years back, people called me—since we have a rather uncommon name—looking for him. My uncle didn't want anything to do with these people, so I told them, "Oh, he retired and moved to Australia. Unfortunately, I don't have his contact info, as we don't get along. He is a real S.O.B.!" I covered for my uncle and steered them completely away from him with misinformation. Saying that we did not get along gave my lie credibility and made me seem like a disgruntled relative who would be happy to give up his uncle. You can do this too, by bragging about moving to, say, Fiji and then moving to Norway.

Then you need to stay hidden:

• **Web sites.** You can't have a site in your name or in a company name that is owned by you.

• **Property.** You can't own any. (You can do things by proxy—open companies, buy homes, register vehicles and cell phones—through a registered agent for a fee, but there's still a possibility that you can be found.)

• **Credit cards.** You can't have any. As we've learned, credit headers are how a lot of public search companies get their data on people, including names, addresses, and Social Security numbers. There's an electronic verification for every transaction you make—from Visa to E-ZPass—or anything that identifies you by name. Yours would be a cash-only life.

• **Bank accounts.** Nope. You'd have to keep your money under a mattress, and—as I teach you in Chapter 7—that's one of the first places burglars look, so good luck with that.

DISAPPEARING ACT CHECKLIST

What to Take
Cash. And lots of it.
Backpack
Prepaid cell phone
Several changes of clothes
   and disguises
Comfortable shoes
Tent (just in case)
Sleeping bag (just in case)
Maps
Compass
Pocketknife

What to Leave
Your credit cards/ATM cards
Your car
Your cell phone

- **Utilities.** As a private investigator, I can come up with your
electric, gas, and cable bills, all from using your name and Social
Security number. So if you try to turn on the electricity in your little
log cabin in the middle of nowhere, I'll still find you.

- **Driver's license.** You can't have one. Virtually all forms of
identification require a registration of some kind.

- **Vehicle.** No way, because you'd have to register it in your name.
You'll have to walk or bike. Still, be mindful of security cameras.
And if you plan to travel by public transportation—rail, subway,
bus—be aware that others are able to see you and you may wind
up inadvertently photobombing someone's vacation photos. A
baseball cap will become your best friend.

- **Employment.** You can't get a job, at least on the books. You'd
have to fill out tax forms and provide personal identification.

- **Social media.** Get rid of all accounts. *All of them.*

- **Change your name.** You'll have to change your name or use an
alias—not legally, but informally. Filing for a legal name change

ARE YOU BREAKING THE LAW?

- You don't want your ex-boyfriend to find you, so you apply for a job using a fake name. **You've just committed a crime!**
- You don't want your wife knowing you're driving up the New York Thruway to see your girlfriend every weekend, so you switch the E-ZPass on your cars. **You've just committed a crime!**
- You think your cover is blown, so you pose as a police officer in order to get yourself out of a jam. **You've just committed a crime!** It's illegal to impersonate someone whose profession requires a license, such as a government official, police officer, doctor, or lawyer.

will lead me right to you. And it is illegal to establish an alias for yourself if you're utilizing it in formal documentation—i.e., filing tax returns, applying for a job. However, if you simply want people to refer to you as *Don Jones* or *Donna Jones*, that's fine. You're not breaking the law as long as you're not defrauding or scamming anyone.

- **Change your appearance.** If you're a redhead, go brunette. Grow a beard. Shave your head. Lose or gain some weight. Dress in vintage instead of designer clothing. The more you can make yourself not look like yourself, the more you can stay hidden.

- **Cultivate new habits.** As we learned in Chapter 3, people tend to hang out in places that they like. However, if you do, you'll be found. It's time to find some new hobbies!

- **Have constant diligence.** Be mindful of where you leave fingerprints and/or bodily fluids. As much as it's possible to reduce digital footprints, you're pretty much stuck with those fingerprints. Prepare to spend the rest of your life looking over your shoulder.

DID YOU KNOW?

- If you are disappearing to escape debts or imprisonment, you could be charged with fraud and imprisoned.
- Staging your own death is a punishable offense.

LEVEL 4: IT'S AN OFF-GRID LIFE FOR US!

Maintaining an off-grid life is nearly impossible if you still want to be a functioning member of society. If you don't properly take care of all those Level 3 duties, any tiny error can show up on a record somewhere and allow someone to find you.

Years ago, an insurance claims person called me up. She said, "Dan, this is going to be a lot of work. My brother has been an alcoholic and a drug addict, and he's missing. He's in his forties, and his wife and kids, who live in Albany, New York, don't know where he is. His last known whereabouts were in Phoenix, but now his phones are disconnected. I think he fell back into the bottle and into the drugs. We want to bring him home. Can you help?"

I thought to myself, *Great, I've got to find a homeless guy.*

I ran a bunch of searches and came up with nothing beyond a certain date, but then I discovered through court records that the guy was arrested for stealing pallets from a warehouse in the Phoenix area. I thought, *Pallets? Why would the guy be going to Home Depot?* And then it hit me. *Maybe he's using them to build himself a shanty.*

I spoke to one of my investigators in Phoenix.

"Where do the homeless people hang out?" I asked.

He said, "There's a dry riverbed where they built a shanty town."

I told him to check it out. The place looked like something out of an episode of *Law & Order: SVU.* The investigator showed the guy's photo around to see if anybody had seen him. After a few tries, a homeless man pointed to the photo and said, "Yeah, I know that guy. He's over there."

TOP ALIASES

These are some of the most common first and last names currently used in the United States. When selecting an alias, choose one from Column A and pair it with one from Column B, and you've just made it that much harder to find you.

First (Column A)	Last (Column B)
Noah	Smith
Sophia	Johnson
Liam	Williams
Emma	Brown
Jacob	Jones
Olivia	Miller
Michael	Davis
Emily	Garcia
James	Rodriguez
Elizabeth	Wilson

We found him, just like that—a guy who had gone virtually off-grid. And if it weren't for that one arrest, we couldn't have done it.

BOY TOY OR BON VOYAGE!

Essentially, you have two choices if you want to disappear:

1. **Become a kept man or woman.** For example, you'd have to find a ninety-year-old in Palm Beach who wants you to be her boy toy. You'll be living in her apartment, driving with her in her car. You're going to have to find someone and piggyback your life onto theirs. You'll have to live in such a way that everything you have is in this person's name, which, if it isn't known, makes it nearly impossible to find you. That might sound exciting and adventurous at first, but you'll really be living like a homeless person with no connections to anything with your name or Social Security number. No real professional can do this for

an extended period of time. It also should be noted that just being with another person can increase your chances of being found. What if you have a falling out? He or she may tattle. You may be better off alone.

2. **Leave the country.** Once you leave the United States, it becomes harder to track you, but are you ready for that? If you're considering an international disappearance, it's important to research the countries in which you plan to live, including any visas or residency cards you may need or what the government regulations are. Also:
    a. Are there communities where you would blend? You don't want to be thought of as the one American guy in town.
    b. Can you speak the language?
    c. Is it a safe place?

There are legitimate reasons to reduce your public profile, and it's important to consider what is driving your wish to fade away. Is it a harassment issue? A cyberstalker? A single bad experience? Fully understand your motivations before committing to a long-term disappearing act. Life is something we all should be running toward, not away from.

7

SAFE HOUSE:
HOW TO PROTECT YOUR HOME, BUSINESS & VALUABLES

Security—whether of a building, an object, or a person—is always a big concern: Is my family safe? My home? My business? My *stuff*? As a private investigator, I employ many physical surveillance and creditability assessment strategies in order to ward off crimes before they happen. Over the course of my career, I have worked as a bodyguard to help protect various celebrities, traveling jewelers, and high-net-worth individuals, as well as precious objects and artwork. In 2005, I even traveled down to Louisiana for two months to help guard the New Orleans Museum of Art after Hurricane Katrina, as well as Tulane University's rare book collection.

The key to protecting your loved ones, your property, and your valuables is to think of security as a series of concentric circles: layer upon layer of insulation. Just as Secret Service agents build

Protect the Family Jewels

concentric circles around the President of the United States—they shut off air space, search Dumpsters for bombs, scour the perimeter for any threats, and circle him with a human shield of agents—you need to provide the necessary layers to keep the bad guys from reaching what's important to you. And that first layer of security is usually your front door.

HOME INVASIONS

Home invasions are entries—usually forceful—into a home with a violent intent to commit a crime against the occupants, such as robbery, assault, murder, rape, and even kidnapping. In other words, unlike most burglaries, these are acts committed by criminals who know there are people inside the homes they enter *and don't care.*

Despite many of the safeguards you might employ to guard against this type of crime, most home invaders usually gain access into a home by walking right through the front door. How? You open it for them.

When considering a move into a new neighborhood:

- Research crime statistics:
  - Contact the local police department—the men and women on the front lines. Know all there is to know about crime in the area.
  - Visit a city's Web site, if there is one, or do an online search for crime and the name of the city.
  - Consult a Web site devoted to crime data, such as neighborhoodscout.com and city-data.com.
- Take several drives through the prospective area at various times of day. Are there bars on the windows of neighborhood businesses? Is it very noisy at night? Is the area located in a flood zone? Near high-voltage wires and high-tension lines? How densely populated is the community? Population-dense areas have an advantage over secluded, rural areas—houses isolated on two acres of property are more at risk for crime than those spaced fifty feet apart.
- Speak to neighbors, store owners, mail carriers. Ask around to get various points of view about the character of the neighborhood and schools.
- Find out if the neighborhood is located near a highway. The closer a town is to main roads, the higher the crime rates usually are, because they offer quick getaway routes.
- Find out if the neighborhood is near a Superfund site? A Superfund site is an uncontrolled or abandoned place where hazardous waste is located and can possibly affect local ecosystems and people. Search epa.gov/superfund/sites.
- Find out if there are sex offenders living in the area. Research the national sex offender registries, especially if you have children, including NSOPW at nsopw.gov or sites such as familywatchdog.us.
- Consider a gated or guarded community, which provides an extra layer of protection against crime.

Security rule #1: A prepared person *never* opens the door for someone that he or she does not know.

This is the number-one mistake people make regarding home security. They have all these fancy shmancy security protocols—including expensive and state-of-the-art alarm systems—but they leave their front door open or unlocked during the day or evening, or when the doorbell rings, they immediately open it without checking to see who is there. They might ask, "Who is it?" and when they hear *Utility man, Can you help me? My car broke down,* or even a voice that is so garbled it sounds like Charlie Brown's elementary school teacher, they open the door anyway. And as soon as they do, they're toast—they've pierced every layer of security they have in one fell swoop.

People tend to feel untouchable or protected when they're at home or in their neighborhoods, surrounded by friends and family and alarm systems, but, unfortunately, the criminals are counting on that. They want to get you at your most vulnerable, your most relaxed. That's why you should always be wary of strangers, whether they ring your doorbell or ring up your groceries.

P.I. GLOSSARY

Case: to study or watch a house, business, store, etc., with the intention of burglarizing it.

If visitors don't seem familiar when you view them through a peephole or door window (both of which you should have), talk to them through the locked door and, if they claim to be salespeople or consultants, ask them to slip ID or a business card into the mail slot. This way, you can confirm their claims by performing an online search for the company. A security-conscious person knows never to trust the information on a card given to him by a stranger. It can be fabricated; phone numbers can lead right to a phone bank set up by the criminals themselves.

A guy came to my house recently at nine o'clock at night. He said he was from the local cable company.

"What do you want?" I shouted through the door.

"Oh, can I talk to you about our cable service?"

"Sorry, I'm happy with my current service."

"You don't even know why I'm here," he said.

"Thank you, and now get off my property. I don't want to talk to you."

The guy was holding up identification the whole time, but I didn't care. Any clown can make a cable company ID on a printer. Many home invaders and burglars pose as:

- Utility workers (gas, electric)
- Salespeople
- Jehovah's Witnesses
- Surveyors
- Public officials (usually during election season/the fall)
- Trick-or-treaters (on Halloween)
- Firefighters
- People asking about a lost pet (sometimes a woman with children in tow)
- Lost people looking for directions
- People seeking some kind of work (handyman, snow shoveler)
- Police officers

Posing as a police officer, in particular, can be an effective pretext for criminals. Most people would open their front door if they believed someone from law enforcement needed to speak to them. That's why criminals pose as cops: for the easy access. Would you really be able to tell if a police officer's badge was real? Probably not. Anyone can buy a badge from a party goods store. And if it *is* authentic, the person may not be, because the badge may have been stolen. (Conversely, the officer may be real and the badge an imposter. Did you know that many New York City cops wear fake badges? They have duplicates, or *dupes*, made in order to put the real one away for safekeeping. Why? If they lose their shield, it could mean lots of paperwork and a hefty penalty!) There are a lot of fake cops out there!

To be sure of his authenticity, you should ask the officer to what precinct he or she belongs so that you can call the precinct directly to verify who the officer is: *Hello, Fourth Precinct? I've got a guy at the door who tells me his name is Officer O'Malley. He says his serial number is 185 . . . That's him? Great, thanks.* And if the officer is in plain clothes, it can be even more difficult to tell the good cops from the bad ones. However, it is within your right to tell the person that you cannot open the door unless you:

- See a marked car
- See a uniformed officer
- Get the officer's tax ID or serial number

A prepared person never lets his guard down. It's like on *Star Trek*: Shields up!

BURGLARIES

A burglary is an entry into a building illegally with intent to commit a crime, especially theft. Unlike home invasions, most burglaries occur when people are *not* home: Burglars will case a neighborhood for homes that look empty for the day or for a string of days, when people are on vacation, for example in order to make their move. Different burglars utilize different strategies. They might ring a doorbell to confirm that no one is around, or stand out of sight or sit in their cars down the block and watch the comings and goings on a particular street to decide on a target.

Although most burglaries are committed during the day when people are at work, there are times, however, when burglars run a

DID YOU KNOW?

Police officers are issued a unique tax ID or serial number. It's never repeated. While their badge or shield numbers may have been handed down to them from their grandfather or from another officer who got promoted to sergeant or left the force, their tax ID and serial number never changes. It's only issued once.

I, Spy

con that's called a *distraction burglary* or *deception burglary*. This type of burglary:

- Is usually conducted in pairs, a burglar and his accomplice
- Is conducted when residents are home
- Often target the elderly. Why?
    - The elderly are more likely to live alone.
    - The elderly are more likely to need assistance with home maintenance, making them vulnerable to those soliciting services for yard work, landscaping, etc.
    - The elderly are more likely to have impaired cognition or judgment and are easy to manipulate.
    - The elderly tend to be cooperative.

The perpetrator of a deception burglary will try to lure a resident out of his or her house with any believable pretext:

"Excuse me, ma'am," a thief, dressed in khakis and a T-shirt, says politely to an elderly woman gardening in her front yard.

"Yes, young man," the woman says, looking up.

"I just wanted you to know that some of the tiles are falling off the side of your house. I wouldn't want you or anyone in your family to become injured."

"Well, how nice of you to tell me," the woman says.

"Here, let me show you," the thief says, keeping sufficient distance from the woman so as not to frighten her. "They're on the other side of the house."

While the woman goes with him and is occupied, an accomplice of the thief will quickly enter the home and pick up any valuables (money, jewelry, documents). It will only take a few minutes.

If you are a victim of a distraction burglary or if you are even suspicious of a strange individual who has approached you, you should call the authorities immediately. You should also pass information (a description of the thieves, the con they pulled) on to neighbors, so that they are aware as well. Social media—Facebook in particular—can be invaluable for helping to spread the word about neighborhood crime. There's no need to let embarrassment keep you from telling others. We all make mistakes.

THWARTING
BURGLARS

- Keep all doors to your home locked, even if you're only in the front yard or walking down the block to slip a letter into a mailbox.
- If you believe a visitor has a legitimate reason to make you leave your home, take your house key, and lock the door behind you.
- Refrain from leaving money, your purse, or your wallet lying around the house. Keep it out of sight.
- Keep good jewelry and small valuables locked in a safe.
- Crosscut or confetti-cut shred all items containing personal information before throwing them into the garbage. You may think that a small appointment card that you received from your dentist is innocuous, but a burglar will discover that card in your garbage, find out you have a dental appointment on a Tuesday in July at three P.M., and clean you out while you're getting a routine cleaning.
- When leaving your home for an extended period of time—vacation, business trip—avoid packing your suitcase into your car in front of passing vehicles or pedestrians. If you have a garage, load up the car inside the garage. If you're parked on the street, try to be inconspicuous. I know people who camouflage their luggage by placing it into laundry bags!
- Always make it seem like your home will be occupied in your absence. When leaving for a trip and getting into a car service vehicle, I'll feign a conversation with my wife, Barbara: *"Hey, Barb, when is Richie coming home? Oh, that's right. He made an arrest and he's working overtime. . . ."* I make sure to mention my son is a cop.

ON-SITE LOCATION SECURITY

Let's say you're having a wedding at a public park or are participating in a trade show event off-site. You'll need to mobilize your security precautions in order to make sure your occasion runs smoothly.

- **Drones.** As with electronic surveillance, from time to time I employ drones for security detail so I can have an eye in the sky. Particularly when I was in the jewelry business on the trade show circuit or working with celebrity clientele, I would need to protect a location. Are there gangs of hoodlums waiting for us down the road? I would launch a drone to find out.
- **Barriers.** Rent barriers, and set up a perimeter to the party or event to have only one way in and out.
- **Invitation only.** Issue invitations, and have someone collect them at the gate, so no uninvited guests can walk in. Remember the movie *Wedding Crashers*? Two guys dressed in suits and crashed parties by blending in! You want the party to be over for these moochers as soon as they arrive!

CONSTANT VIGILANCE

Criminals are most successful when their victims are unsuspecting. That's why the key to home security is to never be unsuspecting. Take advantage of the security systems out there to protect your home. Educate yourself on the best home-security techniques. Information is power. Be ready for anything.

Security rule #2: Thoroughly check out the people you *do* let into your home.

From time to time, we have to let strangers into our homes—handymen, maintenance workers, plumbers, painters, contractors, cable guys, babysitters, nannies, etc. It's not a good idea to just flip through the phonebook or an online directory to find them. You want to make sure these people are not only who they say they are, but that they're reliable and trustworthy:

- Ask friends and family for referrals and recommendations.
- Consult community bulletin boards, if you live in a condo, co-op, or other organized housing. Make sure these boards post only vetted or pre-approved flyers.
- Utilize Web sites that crowdsource recommendations, such as Angie's List.
- Read reviews on Web sites such as Yelp. You read reviews before you buy a book or a computer. Why not before you allow someone to enter your home?
- Pay a visit to your local hardware store or home center for recommendations when looking for a contractor or handyman.
- Check with officials at your local government (town hall, city hall) office that handles building, construction, and permits. Have they seen this contractor around? Is he licensed? Does he do good work? Has he done stuff for other homes in the area? Are there any outstanding complaints or pending legal issues?

Once you finish the screening process:

- Conduct a thorough interview with that person using the creditability assessment techniques we discussed in Chapter 4. Is he or she leaking deception?
- Conduct a preliminary background check to see if anything negative turns up.
- Keep in mind that deception doesn't only show up during an interview or within the early phases of a business relationship. Monitor your worker continuously until the business arrangement

WORST PLACES TO STASH VALUABLES

- Your bedroom sock drawer. I can't tell you how proud some people are to tell me that they've hid all their expensive jewelry in their sock drawer when they go on vacation. That's one of the worst places to hide valuables, because it's one of the first places thieves search. They're going to ransack all the drawers, particularly the top ones, of your bedroom dressers, armoires, and nightstands.
- Under your bed: Terrible. Burglars are going to flip the mattress and search thoroughly under the box spring.
- In a jewelry box. You might as well just put a big blinking neon sign that says *Valuables here! Come one, come all!*

ends, and even then the coast isn't necessarily clear. Teenager Elizabeth Smart was abducted from her bedroom by a handyman who had done work for her parents months and months before. You really have to be vigilant.

Security rule #3: If you can't keep burglars out, slow them down.

The hard truth is that if a criminal *really, really* wants to get into your home or your business or to steal your valuables, he will, one way or another. Eventually. It's just a matter of how long he's willing to work at it. That's why your job, as a home or business owner, is to make his work as difficult as possible by using every system, every gadget, and every scheme you can think of to slow him down.

DID YOU KNOW?

Stickers and signs that read *Warning: These Premises Are Protected by Alarm System* and *Beware of Dog*, even if you have neither, are surprisingly effective. Thieves want the easiest job they can get. If they think your home will be troublesome, they'll pick someone else's.

ALARM SYSTEMS

Basic home security systems, particularly ones that are wired to a central control panel that will activate when windows or doors are opened, can spook burglars from completing their theft. Shining lights and big, blaring noises expose them and usually scare them off. (More advanced—and more expensive—systems will also include fire and carbon monoxide alarms, motion sensors, glass-break detectors, and light and temperature controls.) Ideally, your system should be hooked up to central station, so that once there is a break-in your local police and/or fire department is immediately notified.

However, keep in mind that an alarm system, while a great thing to have, is not foolproof—just as a barking dog is a wonderful deterrent, but shouldn't be your only line of defense. Even with the best alarm systems, there can be a thirty- to forty-five-second delay before the alarm sounds, and it can take anywhere from twenty minutes to three hours for the authorities to respond, depending on how busy they are. House alarm calls often are considered low priority by police and fire departments, because of all the false alarms. If the authorities detect motion sensor activation only, they might think it's your dog or a rat setting off your alarm, whereas front-door activation coupled with a motion sensor raises the priority level.

SECURITY CAMERAS

We discussed security cameras in Chapter 2 as a means of electronic surveillance. They have the same application here, although instead of monitoring a particular subject, they're monitoring all unknown subjects. There are a variety of security

QUICK TIP

If you can't afford to install an alarm system in your home, you can use the Corona or low-budget alarm! Let's say you're a woman, you live alone, and you want to make sure that nobody sneaks into your apartment while you're out. Simply stick a piece of paper or a matchstick into the crevice of where your door meets the doorframe. If the door opens while you're away, the paper will fall out, and you'll know someone has been inside. Make sure the paper or matchstick is in there inconspicuously and securely by bending it so that it sits inside the doorjamb like an *L*. This trick may also be used for hotel room doors, liquor cabinet doors, or bedroom doors.

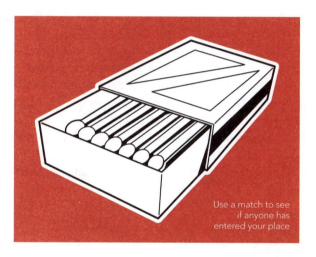

Use a match to see if anyone has entered your place

cameras on the market, and you should choose the one that best meets your needs. Some considerations:

- **Wireless or wired:** Wireless systems, which are flexible and easier to install, are typically used in homes. Large homes and businesses may have more complex requirements that call for wired camera systems.

- **Type/number of cameras:** Do you need weather resistant cameras? Night vision capabilities? As a general rule, homes under 2,000 square feet need approximately four cameras, while larger homes and businesses may require more. Keep in mind that the number of cameras you need will determine the capacity of the digital recording device you need.

- **Remote access:** This will allow you to view your video footage using a smartphone, laptop, or tablet, and also to receive text alerts when something's up. Personally, I find this feature indispensible.

LIGHTING

Strategically placed and timed lighting, both indoors and outdoors, serves as a good burglary deterrent. The last thing an intruder wants is to be identified, and it's easier to do that when you can see his face. There are three types of security lighting:

- **Constant or all-night lighting:** Lighting that shines all the time.

- **Timed lighting:** Lights that turn on and off with the use of timers or apps.

FIVE BEST SPOTS FOR A SECURITY CAMERA

- Front door
- Back/side door
- Basement stairs
- Backyard/side gates
- Off-the-street or hidden first floor windows (or windows attached to a fire escape)

OTHER HOME MUST-HAVES

- Fire extinguishers—in the kitchen, garage, laundry room, and each bedroom of the house
- Smoke alarms—on each floor
- Carbon monoxide detectors—also one per floor
- Flashlights—one in each bedroom
- Water and canned food for three days' worth of meals, just in case there is a blackout, earthquake, zombie apocalypse, or any other unexpected emergency.

- **Motion sensor lighting:** Lighting that only shines when it is triggered by movement.

OUTDOOR LIGHTING

Outdoor lighting comes in a variety of styles, from floodlights, which cast light across a wide area, to path or landscape lighting, which illuminates walkways and stairs. Because standard incandescent bulbs, which are being phased out of use, are too fragile and standard fluorescent bulbs are not designed to withstand the elements, outdoor lighting utilizes three types of bulbs:

- **High Intensity Discharge (HID) bulbs:** HIDs are energy-efficient bulbs that are typically used when you need high levels of intense light over large areas.

- **Halogen bulbs:** Halogen bulbs burn brightly, but also run very hot and can be a burn hazard, which is why they need to be placed at high levels.

- **Light-emitting diode (LED) lights:** LEDs, which are energy efficient, are good sources for constant light. However, keep in mind that an individual LED doesn't offer much brightness—a typical fixture with dozens of strong LEDs might be equivalent to a 40-watt halogen bulb. However, LEDs require less energy than other bulbs and can be used in conjunction with wireless security systems.

INDOOR LIGHTING

For indoor security requirements, there is no need to go out and buy special lighting. You can simply use what you already have.

GLOSSARY

Hardening the target: Strengthening the security of a building in order to protect it from an attack or to reduce the risk of theft.

- When out at night, leave lights on or use timers so that it looks like someone is home. Make sure that some of the lights are in street-facing rooms, so that anyone casing the neighborhood will see them and just keep going.
- If you're going to be out for, say, four nights in a row, leave a different light on each night. Smart lighting control systems and apps, such as those offered by TCP Lighting, allow you to manipulate your lighting even when you are not at home or at your place of business. I use them for my vacation home in Florida as well as my New York residence. Using my smartphone, I can turn TCP lights on and off at will—for example, to turn on at sunset or to dim during the day.

DOORS AND LOCKS

Front doors, as well as back doors and garage doors, need to be sufficiently sturdy to withstand a show of force or manipulation. It's important to use a solid core or metal door for all entrance points, and a high-quality lock, such as a deadbolt, that will resist twisting, prying, and lock-picking attempts. A quality deadbolt will:

- Have a beveled casing to inhibit the use of channel-lock pliers
- Have a *dead latch* to prevent criminals from slipping the lock with a shim or credit card.

QUICK TIP

Sliding glass doors, which are usually secured by latches and not locks, can be one of the weakest entry points into your home. Placing a wooden bat or stick into the track at the bottom of the door can prevent it from opening or at least limit its movement, giving you enough time to call the authorities should there be an attempted break-in.

- Utilize a heavy-duty strike plate (which is the door's weakest point) with long screws.

WEAPONS

The decision to keep a weapon in a home or business is a personal one—and a legal one. Most states require you to have a concealed weapons license if you want to have a gun, for example, in your home for protection. In New York State, you need to be issued a *premises-only* license, which means you can keep the gun in your home (tucked away and out of reach of children and with a required gun lock in place) and use it when you want to go target shooting, but you can't tote it around on a daily basis. (We'll discuss more about weapons use in Chapter 9.)

Sometimes bluffing that you have a weapon is enough to scare off a burglar. A friend of mine has a house in Aruba. He uses constant lighting for the main level grounds. One morning at four o'clock, there was this loud *bang* that sounded like one of his kids dropped the toilet seat. My friend went into their bedroom, but they were asleep. Then he went downstairs and saw a guy with a crowbar trying to break his window.

He started yelling, "Stop, or I'll shoot," and the guy took off.

He said to me later, "Here I am in my underwear in the middle of the night . . . I don't have a bat, I don't have a knife, I don't have anything, but because the lights are so bright out there, the guy

COMMON SENSE
HOME SECURITY TIPS

Dos:

- *Do* keep window-side shrubs trimmed to two or three feet. Often people think that keeping shrubbery tall near windows keeps intruders from being able to get in, but really what you've done is create easy hiding places for them.
- *Do* stop the delivery of all newspapers and mail while you're on vacation, or have a neighbor or friend stop by every day to pick them up.
- *Do* have friends or neighbors park their cars in your driveway to make it look like the home is occupied if you're on vacation.
- *Do* have neighbors shovel snow while you're away and clean off any cars on your property.
- *Do* change your locks immediately if you lose your keys.
- *Do* get insurance for the contents of your home or business. Make sure you have adequate coverage to replace your items if they are stolen or damaged by water, fire, smoke, or whatever peril. Expensive items, such as diamond engagement rings, tennis bracelets, fine arts, and Rolex watches, should be scheduled on your policy. Go over your coverage with your broker annually.
- *Do* keep receipts. I take a picture of every receipt for expensive clothing, electronics, and furniture items. They are in a file called Receipts on my phone. You can make separate folders for each category. Insurance companies love receipts—they are irrefutable

couldn't see me and didn't want to take the chance of getting shot."

The cops wound up catching the guy and arresting him.

All because of a bluff. Trust me. They work. In poker and in security.

proof that you owned an item. Plus, receipts will help if you need warranty service or are ever audited by the tax authorities. (I also send the receipt images to a cloud-based storage company, such as Mozy or Dropbox. This way, if your phone is lost or breaks, you never lose the photos.)

- *Do* take photos of expensive items in your home. I take photos of my house, room by room, and closet by closet, so I have a record of all my jewelry, watches, and fine art. I also take photos of the serial numbers on electronics and watches.
- *Do* have current appraisals for fine art, classic cars, and jewelry. Many people have appraisals from when they purchased an item, but have not updated them. Gold can go from $800 an ounce to $1,200 an ounce very quickly, meaning that you would be 25 percent underinsured if you are using old gold prices.

Don'ts:

- *Don't* display your name on your mailbox or door. Doing so allows any passerby to know your name—conmen may pretend that they know you if they follow you away from your home— and gives criminals easy access to your telephone number.
- *Don't* leave notes for family members or service people on the door.
- *Don't* post plans for being away on open social media accounts.
- *Don't* leave very expensive valuables or important or irreplaceable documents at home. Put them in a safety deposit box.
- *Don't* forget about flood insurance. Many of my neighbors on Long Island had no flood insurance when Superstorm Sandy hit. They took a real beating financially for damage to their homes and contents. Remember, security, proper documentation, and insurance don't cost—they pay!

STASHING VALUABLES

It's important to remember that all your layers of defense—alarm systems, security camera systems—can be breached. Therefore, it's a good idea to create extra layers of protection using a little common sense and creativity.

Buy a safe. Get into the habit of safeguarding your valuables. Purchase a small safe that can be bolted into the beams of a wall or floor in your home or business—a safe is no good to you if a thief can run away with it on his back. And make sure it is installed in an area that is out of the way for a criminal, but accessible to you. Buy a good quality one—it will last you a lifetime and is an excellent investment!

Divide and conquer. Don't keep all your valuables in one basket. Scatter them around—place jewelry under a bathroom sink with the cleaning supplies and stick your passport under the kitchen dish rack. A burglar is only in a home for a few minutes, and he is going to grab what he can before running away. Keep a little bit here and a little bit there. Like a squirrel, you don't want to leave all your nuts in one place.

Leave bait. Thieves may not be sure of what they're looking for. They just know that they want to leave with *something*. So give them something. Rubber-band a hundred dollars' worth of cash—in tens and twenties—and stick it in an entryway drawer. Buy yourself a costume-jewelry bracelet, and place it on the top of your bedroom dresser. Leave an old laptop that you don't even use anymore right on the kitchen table. If the criminals leave your house with a hundred bucks, a bracelet, and a laptop, they'll think they hit a home run! Meanwhile, all the good stuff is hidden elsewhere. Burglars are probably only going to look until they find something they think is valuable, and once they do, they'll be satisfied. Just a little bait will keep them from digging further.

Stow valuables in improbable places. Most criminals will head toward the same places to find valuables—upstairs bedrooms, drawers, safes, filing cabinets. It saves them time and usually yields the most loot. That's why you should put your important items in unlikely places: cereal boxes, mixed nut canisters, inside the

Hide your valuables in a book.

pages of a book (not the Bible—thieves love the Bible!) on your bookshelf. You even can use a utility knife to cut out indentations in a book or two to hide your valuables inside. A friend of mine bought some jewelry from me in the eighties, and he had his money wrapped in aluminum foil—it was ice cold! He said, "I keep it in my freezer under the steaks." Who's going to ransack your freezer for cash? Not very many.

DID YOU KNOW?

There are products on the market that resemble beer cans, soda cans, soup cans, cleanser cans, and shaving cream canisters, but they are empty and have a secret compartment for stashing personal and important items. Some of these look-alike containers are even

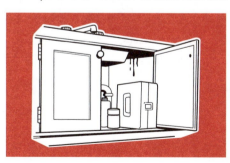

weighted to feel full! My son had a fake can of WD-40 in his college apartment. That is where he kept his valuables— under the kitchen sink with all his other household products.

Bury. Again, thieves don't want to stick around. They want to be quick. Therefore, if you bury your valuables somewhere in the house—at the bottom of a pile of shoes in the closet or at the back of your pantry behind the boxes of macaroni—the longer it will take them to find anything.

Bolstering every layer of your security—from installing an alarm system to hiding your cash—can greatly reduce your risk of becoming a victim of crime in your home or business. Simple procedures and behavior modifications, while not fail-safe, can make you a less appealing target. Nobody wants to be a victim. Remember, criminals who successfully breach your security protocols may steal more than just your possessions. They may rob you of your peace of mind. And, once violated, that is one of the hardest things to restore. ■

8

IDENTITY THEFT: HOW TO PROTECT YOUR PRIVACY

I dentity theft, also known as *identity fraud*, refers to crimes in which someone wrongfully obtains and uses another person's personal data to defraud, defame, or deceive, typically for economic or financial gain. It has become one of the biggest and most problematic crimes taking place today. With the ease and accessibility of technology, any document or transaction has the potential to be a scam. There are various kinds of identity theft, including:

- **Financial identity theft:** This can occur when credit reports and bank accounts are breached, and is the type of identity theft with which people are most familiar.

- **Insurance identity theft:** This is big money. Medical care is one of the hottest commodities in the United States today.

- **Medical identity theft:** Scammers visit hospitals, emergency rooms, and pharmacies to receive care and prescriptions, all on your dime.

- **Social Security identity theft:** Social Security numbers can be sold to those needing citizen statuses, such as illegal immigrants, along with driver's license identification numbers.

- **Income tax fraud.** Scammers use your identity and file a false return, claiming a refund. *They* receive the refund, while you get stuck being audited. And with e-filing, they can, while sitting in their underwear, transfer the funds straight into their bank account. Then they withdraw the money and close the account.

Thieves conduct identity theft, both online and off. Be ready for them. To protect your personal privacy, adopt the same vigilance as you would to protect your home and your valuables.

DUMPSTER DIVING

You can tell a lot about a person by what he or she throws out—more than you realize. As we discussed in Chapter 5, garbage retrieval is one of the ways people can get a hold of your stuff—legally. That's why you need to trash your trash!

Most people think that only discarded items showing their name, address, telephone number, date of birth, or Social Security number is unsafe, but the truth is that any personal information is desirable to an identity thief. This includes seemingly innocuous documents such as correspondence from your children's school, your husband's company, the stores where you like to shop, and where you bank. For example, if you receive a brochure from Bank of America, and a thief discovers it in your trash, he now knows where you bank and can prank you:

WHAT
SCAMMERS
ARE LOOKING FOR

- Copies of your checks
- Credit card or bank statements
- Personal correspondence
- Retail store brochures and mailings
- Anything that bears your name, address, and telephone number
- Anything that tells them where you go and what you like to do

"Hello, Mrs. Jones, my name is Sarah, and I'm calling from Bank of America to make sure you received our flyer regarding your preferred customer status dated March 24th. We are so thankful for your business that we'd like to make you an even better offer! Let me look up your account, so I can see the best rate that you qualify for. Would you kindly confirm the last four digits of your Social Security number for me?"

Seems credible, doesn't it? Meanwhile, the thief may already have the other digits of your Social, because those numbers can be obtained on some commercially available databases and even some public records filings that just redact the last four. All they have to do is piece all the numbers together. The more believable a person sounds, the more likely you are to fill in the blanks for her.

To foil Dumpster divers, crosscut-shred, or confetti-shred, all personal documents or papers. A crosscut shredder uses two contra-rotating drums to cut rectangular, parallelogram, or diamond-shaped shreds, and, as mentioned in Chapter 5, will destroy documents in a way that is virtually impossible to recreate. Shred your personal and junk mail on a regular basis, while you're watching television or reading the Sunday paper. Make it part of your routine.

MAIL SCAMS

Old-school conmen still use snail mail to defraud someone. They will:

- Issue fake checks and money orders
- Offer fraudulent financial opportunities in the form of lottery and work from home scams.
- Offer fraudulent refunds from banks or the IRS

As technology has improved, so have mail scams! Publishing software applications such as Adobe InDesign or Photoshop, purchased online or at any office supply store, allow scammers to make posters, brochures, and flyers that look like the real deal. It is important to scrutinize all correspondence that you receive by mail. Consider:

- Does this offer seem too good to be true?
- Is it badly written?
- Is the return address correct and complete?
- Is it addressed to you directly or to Dear Resident or Dear Sir or Madam?
- Does the company or organization exist? Can you find it on Google Maps?
- Are greetings and closings correct? Does it say Yours Sincerely?
- Does it require you to send money or write a check?

When in doubt, always call or contact a company directly. Also, check to see where the company is headquartered, and contact that state's secretary of state and/or division of corporations to make sure it is a legitimate entity.

SHOULDER SURFING

In addition to watching you at home, criminals will follow you around as you run errands or travel to and from work. Sometimes they get close enough to glean credit card or bank card information—they will *shoulder surf*, or look over your shoulder,

DID YOU KNOW?

Mail theft can be just as damaging as home theft. Criminals can steal your mail right from your mailbox in order to scam you. For example, if a thief steals your credit card statement from your mailbox while you're at work, he can call up your credit card company and pretend to be you:

Representative: "Good morning. Thank you for calling ABC Credit Card Company. How can I help you?"

Criminal: "Hello, my name is Sam Smith, and I'm in the process of moving and lost my wallet, and I'm worried about all my credit card information."

Representative: "Don't worry, Mr. Smith. We can help you with that."

Criminal: "I'm moving tomorrow. My new address is 555 Main Street in Des Moines. Do you think you can overnight me a replacement card?"

Representative: "We certainly can, Mr. Smith. You'll receive your new card tomorrow."

The next day the scammer, who has been watching your home for weeks, knows you'll be at work all day and that you don't get very many package deliveries. When the overnight shipment truck shows up, the scammer makes sure to be standing near the home's front door and runs to meet the driver.

"For Sam Smith, right?" he asks the driver, looking relieved. "I've been waiting for this! Sorry that I need to rush you, but I have to leave. I'm late for an appointment."

He signs for the package and not only does he have your credit card, but the credit card company now thinks that your address has changed to an address he has designated.

If you suddenly stop receiving statements from your bank or credit card company, it's a good idea to contact those institutions to make sure your address hasn't been changed or your information compromised. And check bank account balances regularly—if they seem out of whack, dig out your withdrawal receipts and statements, and contact your lending institution. To avoid mail scams of this type altogether, opt for paperless statements.

TIPS TO THWART PICKPOCKETS

- Use purses and backpacks that zip.
- Carry backpacks on the front of your person in crowds.
- Dress down. Pickpockets only go after people they think have something worth stealing.
- Keep credit cards and valuables out of easily accessible spots, such as your back pocket.
- Try not to carry more than one credit card, if possible.

as you punch your access code or password into a self-checkout machine or an automated teller machine, or they will take a quick photo of your card with their smartphone as you slide it in and out of a card reader. While you're out and about, scammers also will try to eavesdrop on your phone conversations in order to obtain your credit card number if, say, you're trying to reserve a hotel room or concert tickets. Shoulder surfing is most prevalent in crowded places or close quarters where it's easy to observe, such as the ATM vestibule of a bank. Make a point to always be aware of who is around you when speaking on the phone, and shield a keypad or document (eyes on your own paper!) with one hand while using the other to input information.

Shield the keypad to hide your PIN when using an ATM.

DID YOU KNOW?

Whenever you are asked to enter a numbered passcode or PIN, such as onto the keypad of an ATM, you should always touch other numbers after you finish your transaction. There is thermal-imaging software available that allows scammers to place their smartphones or other devices over the keypad after you leave, revealing your heat signature and alerting them to the specific numbers you pressed. From that signature, they can figure out your password, because you've narrowed down the numbers for them. Therefore, if you touch additional numbers, or all of them, your heat signature becomes meaningless.

ATM SKIMMERS

Scammers will install hidden devices, called overlays, onto ATMs that enable them to swipe your account information once you insert your card and to transmit that information to a nearby computer for future fraudulent use. It is very important that you pay attention to the condition and design of the ATM you use. These overlays can be inserted onto any type of unit that processes ATM, debit, or credit cards, such as public transit, gas station, and movie ticket machines. The overlays are wafer-thin and may not be noticeable unless you're looking for them.

MONITORING SOFTWARE

Monitoring software, also known as computer surveillance software, observes and tracks your computer usage. As we discussed in Chapter 2, it can be used for electronic surveillance legally if you install it on a computer that you own—for example, to see if your teenagers are surfing porn. However, many times monitoring software is used illegally and with nefarious intent:

- **Malware:** Software that is intended to damage or disable your computer.

- **Spyware:** Software that allows scammers to monitor and steal your computer activities by transmitting your data to their hard drive.

- **Keylogging:** Software that fraudulently records every keystroke you make on your computer, usually to gain access to passwords and other confidential information.

The best way to thwart these types of programs is to utilize the services of an identity theft protection company, such as LifeLock. For only a few bucks a month, identity theft protection companies will safeguard your credit, your financial data, and your good name. You also should purchase a comprehensive antivirus program, such as McAfee or Norton, which can act as your virtual personal bodyguard—it will detect monitoring software or viruses found on Web sites you visit. (The monthly costs are the same as those for a monthly latte—and these programs contain fewer calories! Don't be cheap. It's worth it.)

PEER-TO-PEER FILE SHARING

Peer-to-peer (P2P) file sharing is a popular way to exchange movies, photos, music, and documents online. How it works is you download software that connects your computer to other computers that run the same software—potentially connecting millions of computers at a time. As you would imagine, this opens up your computer to lots of strangers and puts the information stored on your computer at risk—either for viruses, monitoring software, or identity theft. (If you are a business owner, be aware of the security implications of using P2P file-sharing software; you need to protect the personal and sensitive information of your employees and customers.) It is important to take great care when using P2P file-sharing applications by installing a reputable security and antivirus program and by understanding how the application works and how you can limit your exposure.

PHISHING

Phishing is the attempt to acquire sensitive and personal information such as usernames, passwords, credit card numbers, and Social Security numbers, by masquerading as a trustworthy entity via Web site or e-mail. It is a subset of *spoofing* (see box, page 148). (*SMSishing* is considered the attempt to acquire information via text messages to a mobile device.) Think of an e-mail sender line as you would the Caller ID of your telephone: it announces who is trying to contact you. Scammers will disguise themselves behind credible-looking names or designations in order to gain access to your personal data. Like snail mail scams, phishing scams have become more sophisticated, but there are often signs that something is amiss:

P.I. GLOSSARY

Spam: a disruptive online message, often sent as an e-mail, that offers irrelevant or inappropriate messages to a large number of recipients. It may or may not seek to defraud you, but it can definitely entertain you. Viagra, anyone?

- You are receiving customer notification from a retailer or company, but you are not a customer of that particular retailer or company.
- The e-mail is not addressed to you. Instead, it is addressed to an unknown e-mail address or *undisclosed recipients*.
- There is an ominous warning of some kind: *If you don't respond in two days, then we will shut down your account permanently!*

SPOOFING VERSUS PHISHING

There is often confusion between the terms *spoofing* and *phishing*:

Spoofing
Definition:
Spoofing is when scammers pretend to be someone else in order to trick you into doing something you wouldn't ordinarily do, such as click on a link that will download malware or spyware onto your computer. It is often done with the intent to defraud, cause harm, or wrongfully obtain something of value, but not always. Sometimes, people are just messing with you.

Phishing
Definition:
Phishing is an attack in which scammers try to trick you into divulging personal or sensitive information resulting in a financial gain for them. They are *fishing* for your information.

Masquerade as a trustworthy entity: Yes

Masquerade as a trustworthy entity: Yes

Example: "Dear Mr. Ribacoff: Our records indicate that your computer has been infected with malicious software. Please click the following link to address this matter." (Following the e-mail directions results in the downloading of malicious software onto my computer.)

Example: "Dear Mr. Ribacoff: Our records indicate that there was unlawful activity on your credit card. Please click the following link and provide your username and password to remedy this situation as soon as possible to prevent identity theft." (Following the e-mail directions results in identity theft.)

Illegal? Yes, if the intent is to defraud/cause harm

Illegal? Yes

Identity theft? Not necessarily

Identity theft? Yes

- Misspellings, improper punctuation, and awkward phrasing might be present. Virtually no e-mail features perfect grammar, but phishing scams often have more than their fair share of errors.

If you suspect that you have received a fraudulent electronic communication:

- Do not reply or respond directly.
- Do not click on any provided link.
- Do not download or open an attachment.
- Do not cut and paste links into your browser.

Instead, do contact the organization in a separate e-mail, by phone, or through its official website.

VISHING

Vishing, or *voice phishing*, is the attempt to acquire sensitive and personal information via voice calls made to a landline or mobile phone. Criminals go to great lengths to convince you that they are legit, all to get your personal identifiers: *We're updating your records. I'm calling from your gas company and want to verify your Social.* Again, a security-savvy person will not give out any information over the phone—no matter how credible the person sounds. Remember, banks and credit card companies should already have your information and don't need you to recite it back to them. Instead:

- Tell the person you will call him back, and then call the number on the back of your credit card, bill, or statement. Sometimes scammers will offer to give you an 800 number to save you money—how thoughtful of them!—but, again, those numbers lead to fraudulent people or organizations.
- Tell the person to put the call into your record and that you will call the organization back at another time. When you do follow up, using the numbers on your credit card, bill, or statement, ask the representative if there was a notation in your record of the previous call. If he or she says no, then you know that call was a scam.
- As a test, offer a fake account number. If the person says, "Yep, that's correct. You're in," hang up and call the authorities.

IF YOU SUSPECT THAT YOU'VE BEEN A VICTIM OF IDENTITY THEFT

- Place a fraud alert with the credit-reporting companies: Equifax, Experian, and TransUnion. It is free and can make it harder for an identity thief to open more accounts in your name.
- Request a copy of your credit reports. A fraud alert entitles you to a free copy from each of the three credit reporting companies.
- File an Identity Theft Report with the Federal Trade Commission as well as a complaint with your local police department.

A WORD ON PASSWORDS

A password or passcode is an important line of defense against identity theft. Every account you have—cell phone, bank, credit card, alarm company—should require a password for access. This is an extra layer of protection beyond those security questions companies like to ask, such as *What was your first pet's name?* or *What's your favorite sports team?* If your accounts are not passcoded, you should call up the company you use and say, "I want to passcode my account. I'm having problems with my husband. I want to make sure he doesn't scam me!"

When selecting a password, far too many people make the mistake of choosing something personal—the name of their dog or the name of a child, for example—because it's easy for them to remember. The problem is, it's also easy for scammers to figure out. Do you know how many people know the name of my dog, Harley? There are more photos of Harley than Kim Kardashian on the Internet. If I use Harley as my password, I may as well write out a check for my checking account balance payable to Scammer.

Some password tips:

- **Make your password ridiculously stupid.**
  Frenchtoastandketchup. Mybananaopenapplesauce. Who's going to think of that?

- **Don't use real words.** *blickypuckanow.*

- **Include numbers, symbols, and capital letters.** And capitalize the middle letters of words, not just the first one. *opEnsacRament.*

- **Store passwords where people cannot gain ready access to them.** There are apps on the market called password keepers that protect your password information for you. They are safer than writing a password down on a piece of paper and keeping it in your wallet (which can be stolen) or scribbling it on the inside of your kitchen cabinet (which can be found by a burglar).

- **Change your password regularly.** People get complacent and may have the same password for the last thirty years. However, it's a good idea to change your password on a regular basis— every six months to a year. Of course, if you think there's been a breach of any sort, or if you've clicked on a link that may have compromised your electronic device, run a virus scan, and change your password from another device, just in case spyware is present on the infected machine.

SIX WORST TYPES OF PASSWORDS

- Pet names
- Birthdates
- Digits in your address/phone number

- Children's names
- Anniversaries
- School names

BUSINESS SMARTS

- Vary your passwords—you should need a different one to access each employee's workstation.
- Keep all filing cabinets with important documents locked and secured.
- Shred all documents and drafts of documents. (Cleaning crews at night can be paid to steal information by competitors or scammers.)
- Educate every employee in your organization, from the boardroom to the mailroom, about identity theft. They should understand the value and sensitivity of the information to which they have access as well as how to protect it.
- Create a corporate culture that takes security seriously. A good example should be set from the top.

- **Keep the blinds closed** when typing in a password at home, and cover your computer screen if you're in a public place. People are opportunists. You never know.

ONLINE SHOPPING

There's no denying the ease and convenience of online shopping. Who wants to go schlepping through the snow or rain to buy a Valentine's Day gift when all you have to do is click a few buttons on your computer and you're done? However, online shopping does have its hazards, so it's important to shop smart—this means not only knowing the best Web sites to buy shoes, but also how to avoid the perils of identity theft:

- Make sure the retail stores with which you do business are legitimate. Always manually type URLs and e-mail addresses.
- Always use a credit card rather than a debit card. Credit cards will protect you against fraud. With debit cards, it's more difficult to get back lost funds.

- When reviewing items on credit card bills, look for incremental purchases—one dollar here, two dollars there. Thieves will test stolen credit card numbers with small purchases to see if the card number is good.
- Use a virtual credit card, which is a single-use credit card number usually generated by your credit card issuer. Virtual credit card numbers can only be used once—they expire after about a month, if not used—and can offer peace of mind, particularly when shopping on a Web site for the first time.
- Use Apple Pay, Google Wallet, or similar mobile-payment software. Nowadays, there's no need to go searching for credit card numbers in order to pay for a purchase. There is software available that offers contactless payment technology—all you have to do is hold your smartphone near a contactless reader, tap, and pay. As soon as you make a payment, you will receive a notification, which means you will also be notified if anyone else is fraudulently trying to make a payment using your account.

Unfortunately, even with all the best-laid security protocols, your information may still be at risk if there is a data breach at any of the businesses with which you do business. Scammers will find a vulnerability wherever they can. The best you can do is take care of your end. Educate yourself. Install protective services. Be mentally prepared. As a private investigator, I use ruses all the time to extract information. Don't fall for people like me. ■

9

BACK OFF, PAL:
HOW TO PROTECT YOURSELF

There are various risks that you face just being anywhere. Whether you're in the city or in the sticks, thousands of miles away from home or down the street, dangerous situations can present themselves. Ex-boyfriends. Ex-wives. Former employees. Complete strangers. Anyone can pose a threat or intimidate, so it's important to always be prepared. Just like the Boy Scouts.

There are usually indicators that your safety is in jeopardy—that guy at the deli is being especially pesky, a woman keeps popping up on your route when you go for a run, your rabbit's been boiled. You get the idea. You'll have an inkling that *something* isn't right, even if you're not sure what that something is. That's your human intuition talking to you.

Back in caveman days, if you saw a saber-toothed tiger, you ran. No questions asked. Today, you see what amounts to a saber-toothed tiger, and you think,

A WORD
ABOUT RESTRAINING
ORDERS

When it comes to personal protection, many times restraining orders are useless. Why? Because bad guys don't abide by the law. Sure, a decent guy, a businessman maybe, who got into a little tiff with his wife will respect the order, but a boyfriend who's been in jail ten times? No way. We see this on *The Steve Wilkos Show* all the time. Restraining orders offer an extra layer of protection, but unfortunately many times they offer a false sense of protection as well.

I'm in a good neighborhood, nothing is going to happen, and then all of a sudden you get clonked on the head. People kill their human intuition with rationalization, and it knocks the common sense right out: *I don't have a good feeling about walking down this street or cutting through this dark, empty housing development, but what are the chances of something happening? I'll do it anyway.* Nice going, genius. A security-conscious person would have walked an extra block out of her way to maintain her safety.

Personal protection consists of three principles:

- **Constant awareness**
- **Scanning your environment**
- **Taking proper precautions**

CONSTANT AWARENESS

Some people are oblivious. You could follow them for a hundred miles, and they wouldn't notice. With others, the second you walk behind them, they're alert. They have constant awareness. If you were a stalker, whom would you follow? Mr. Ignorant or Mr. Cognizant? Exactly. You can't walk around like everything's rosy all

PERSONAL
THREAT LEVELS

White: Your threat level should never be white. There are always foreseeable threats.

Yellow: An average day. Maintain a routine state of alertness.

Orange: A heightened state of alertness due to a specific focal point—a person or vehicle that has raised your suspicion.

Red: Code red! Danger detected!

the time with your headphones in your ears, because situations change based on who you are, where you are—or even when you are. For instance, in the summertime, crime escalates, especially street crime. You've got more kids outside with nothing to do, so you're going to have issues. Plus, your jewelry, your smartphones, your valuables—everything is more exposed in the summer and not hidden behind scarves and long sleeves. It's time to raise your level of awareness. And when you suspect that you're being harassed, followed, or stalked, you need to raise your level of awareness that much more.

Just as the government has its yellow, orange, and red threat levels, as a human being you need to have those as well. I am working with a client whose daughter's boyfriend is staying at his house because he's taking some classes. My client said his daughter's head over heels for the guy and that he likes him too—he's a nice kid, and his father is a police detective. Sounds like a match made in heaven, right? But guess what? Systematically, money has been missing from my client's house. Then my client decides to check his wife's jewelry box and the pills in the medicine cabinet. They're also gone. I told him he should have called me the first time something disappeared, and I would have installed surveillance cameras. "Yeah," he said, "but I didn't want to believe it." He wanted to believe this kid was a *nice boy*—after all, he's polite and mows the lawn. Meanwhile, the runt is stealing. If my client would have raised his level of awareness the first time something went missing, we could have solved the problem much sooner.

SCANNING YOUR ENVIRONMENT

Arson, acts of terrorism, street crime—these are all dangers that we face in today's world. Therefore, you have to be mindful of your surroundings not only for your own personal safety, but for the safety of others (we'll talk more about public safety in Chapter 10). I see so many people who are talking or texting on their phone, totally oblivious and preoccupied. They concentrate on what they're doing versus what's around them, and it's only a matter of time until that gets them into trouble. The human mind can only do a certain number of tasks at a time before it overloads itself, so it's important to find a way to focus on your personal safety in addition to Twitter or Words with Friends or what you're having for dinner. Think tactically:

- **Locate all exits.** Whenever you enter a building, familiarize yourself with the location of all the nearest entrances and exits. Just like on a plane. You always want to know what's available to you as part of your scan process.

- **Use your peripheral vision.** When I'm walking around a city or on a main, busy street, I am always using my peripheral vision. I might be pretending that I'm looking in a store window when I'm actually utilizing the reflection to see who's behind me.

- **Plan scenarios.** Ask yourself: *If something happens right now—a burglary, a gang war—how would I find safety?* Would you have a plan? Would you know what to do?

TAKING PROPER PRECAUTIONS

On an average day, your personal threat level is condition yellow. Even if you're sitting in a police station, you don't know if a lunatic's

TEAM SCHEMES

When I was in the diamond business in Manhattan, the typical scam was to use teams or decoys to steal jewelry. If thieves saw you walking down Forty-Seventh Street with a bag, they assumed that you were a traveling salesman and might plant a decoy in your path—a lady with a baby, an attractive woman, a young boy. The decoy would say, "Mister, you have ketchup on your jacket" or "Mister, you dropped money," and then, while you were distracted, a second person would knock you over, grab your bag, and run. Remember, the bad guys are not always alone or always recognizable—your ex-boyfriend may have hired others to do his stalking for him—so it's important to be aware of any stranger, no matter how nicely dressed.

---

coming in with an AK-47, so it's always best to maintain a routine state of alertness. It's no different from keeping a jack in your car; you want to be prepared. However, if you suspect that you're being followed or stalked, your everyday state of awareness needs to be raised and accompanied by a call to action:

- **Seek help.** Obviously, locate a police officer. That's what the police are there for. They don't charge, and you pay taxes, so don't be scared to approach one. If there are no officers around, duck into a restaurant or store, or a place where there are people. Tell the clerk, security guard, somebody bigger than you who looks respectable, "This guy is following me." Most people are willing to help somebody in distress. If you're in your car and you feel like you're being tailed, dial 911, and give the operator as much information as you can: *I'm being followed by a gray BMW. I can see the New York license plate. The first three letters are AIY.* You should keep yourself moving so as not to get blocked or boxed in. Drive to the nearest precinct, if you know where that is, or someplace public. If you're on the highway, go to a rest area with restaurants and a gas station.

DISGUISES,

If you sense you're being followed as you walk down the street, try altering your appearance on the fly. The following, or a combination of the following, can garner you enough time to hop onto a subway car, dart into a store, get lost in a crowd, or otherwise reach safety.

- Slip on a pair of sunglasses or prescription glasses.
- Place a baseball cap or any other hat, preferably with a long or wide brim, onto your head to obscure your face and the back of your head.
- Affix a fake moustache to your upper lip (they work!). Or, if you're desperate and your stalker is far enough away, dig a marker or pen out of your purse or pocket and try drawing one across your upper lip.
- Remove any bright or red-colored accessories, such as scarves, ties, or sashes, and either carry them, place them in a bag, or lose them.
- Strip down. Take off your outer garments and carry them, particularly if your clothing underneath is a completely different color. Or remove a business shirt and walk around in a T-shirt or undergarment, if you're wearing one.
- Change your hairstyle:
  - Place your hair into a ponytail with a rubber band, or put a scarf around your head.
  - Comb your hair in a different direction. I like to comb mine back guido-style. Mess it up, wet it, and make it stand up

- **Alter your schedule.** The more predictable you are, the easier you are to find. Leave an hour earlier for the office. Use a different building exit. Take a later train home.

- **Vary your route.** Mix it up! Cross the street. Stop, look in a store window, and start again. If you find that a certain someone is always there—you're changing your pace, walking fast, walking slow, and he is too—seek help. Same if you're driving. When I

IN A PINCH

like a Mohawk. Change your part—you'd be surprised how different you look if you part your hair down the middle instead of to the side. Or try brushing your hair forward, like the crazy one from *The Breakfast Club*, to cover your face.

- Alter the clothing you are wearing. Roll up your sleeves. Turn up the collar on your jacket or shirt. Turn your jacket inside out. Pull up the bottom of a long raincoat, so that it only reaches your waist. Roll up your pants so that they resemble capri pants or shorts. Use what you've got!

- Hold up a prop—such as an umbrella, a newspaper, or a clipboard. This can change your look and be used to obscure your face. Or hold up your phone to your ear, and try to cover as much of your face as possible with your hand and arm.

- Walk closely to another person who is bigger than you and use him as cover.

- Stuff cotton, wax, or chewing gum between your cheek and teeth, lips, and gums. A protruded jaw can change the whole contour of your face.

- Stick a bandage on your cheek. It may draw strangers' attention, but the one person who is looking for you might walk right by.

- Change your posture, your walk, your attitude. Stoop, hunch, whatever you can do to not look like you. However, whatever position you choose, always be prepared to run.

---

was a jewelry salesman and traveled across the country, I was often followed, so I'd conduct counter-surveillance. I never would drive directly from jeweler to jeweler. I would go through a parking lot, make a U-turn, drive around the block, and look for a tail. These days, however, a stalker has the ability to GPS your car—which, as discussed in Chapter 2, is illegal. If you suspect that your car has a tracking device—with the use of magnets, the gadgets are usually stuck to the bottom of your vehicle—either:

- Use a friend's car.
- Take your car to a gas station or auto garage, and tell the mechanic, "I think somebody put a tracking device on my car. Can you look at it? I'll give you ten bucks." He's bound to help you out.

- **Change your appearance.** I had a client in the diamond business who was crazy paranoid. She thought people were following her. *All the time.* I don't know why. She would come in one day dressed in this big, floppy hat and sunglasses, and then the next day you'd see her wearing a blond wig. She was changing her look constantly. To throw off a tail, you need to do the same thing. Utilize the same strategies we discussed in Chapter 1; they work just as well on the other side of a physical surveillance. Also, refrain from wearing any signature items—big-rimmed sunglasses, your coveted Indiana Jones fedora. They give you away. When I am hired to conduct a surveillance, a wife might send me a photo of a middle-aged guy who looks like every other guy out there, because everybody gets the same haircut, has the same suit. So I'll ask, "What does your husband have that's unusual?" One time, a wife told me, "He'll always carry a brown Louis Vuitton briefcase and wear a gold Rolex watch." Later, when I saw a guy with the briefcase and watch, I knew it was him!

- **Dress appropriately.** If you're going to wear a pencil skirt and four-inch heels with a platform when you think your boyfriend is stalking you, you're probably not going to outrun him.

- **Protect your personal space.** This is very important. The space between you and another person should be at least an arm's length—two arm's lengths, if you can. Why? Personal space gives you reaction time. Think of when you're driving a car and someone is right up your tail. If you hit the brakes, *bang.* The car is going to smash into you, because it doesn't have enough time to stop. Same with personal space—if a person is walking too closely to you, you have less time to react if he or she wants to physically assault you. Distance, on the other hand, gives you more reaction time and allows you to take action. Of course, in metropolitan areas, personal space may be at a premium, but there are ways to create personal space when necessary. For instance, if somebody comes up to you in a crowded city or room and says, "Hey, lady," you can:

- Take a step back. This creates the personal space you need to react.
- Stand sideways. This adds a layer of personal space and throws the other person off balance, so that if he tries to grab you, you can sidestep him.
- Walk faster and toward a destination—the nearest exit, a store, the subway, etc.

- **Make a scene.** You shouldn't be afraid to scream or make a commotion when you feel immediately threatened. The police aren't likely to arrest you for jumping up and down like a lunatic. And when you're drawing attention to yourself, the bad guys lose the element of surprise, and their natural reaction is flight.

Need to lose someone in a crowd? Look up at a building, point, and yell, "Oh my God!" Everyone will look up and scan the building for several seconds, giving you time to scurry away!

"TOO'S" A CROWD

If you meet people at a club, in a bar, or online, how do you know they're on the up and up? Are they who they say they are? Or do they have something to hide? In addition to those signs of deception we discussed in Chapter 4, keep in mind that bad things often come in *too's*:

- Is this person being *too* friendly? You're at the airport and a stranger, who *happens* to be going in the same direction as you, offers to share a cab to save time or money. Meanwhile, he or she may be trying to find out where you live (remember the film *Taken*?) or rob you. It's best to always decline an offer from a stranger.

- Is this person standing *too* close to me? Remember what Sting said: Don't stand so close to me! Maintain that personal space.
- Is this person asking *too* many personal questions? *What kind of car do you drive? Where do you go to school? What do your parents do?* He or she may be fishing for information to see if you're a good person to abduct or if you've got some expensive goodies he can steal from your person or your house. Always downplay your responses until you can feel the person out.
  - If you live in an upper-class neighborhood, say you live in a middle-class neighborhood.
  - If your father is a one-percenter, say he works two jobs to make ends meet.

  You can always tell the person—if he turns out to be trustworthy—the truth later. Remember, it's easier to correct up than down. For example, if you say you are the CEO of a company, but you're really a fry cook, people might get pissed when they learn the truth. But if people think you're a fry cook only to find out you're a CEO, they are pleasantly surprised. Nobody is pissed.
- Don't get *too* drunk, particularly if you're alone, so that you lose the ability to control your own actions.
- Don't have sex with someone who is *too* drunk or high. The next day, that person can say she was impaired and that you assaulted or raped her. I have had many cases like this— especially in colleges!
- Don't be *too* scared or shy to ask people for a copy of their driver's license if you plan to go to their house, have them come over to your house, or go anywhere else where you are leaving your friends. Take a picture of the ID and text it to a friend or family member. If they won't let you, don't leave with them! An honest person will understand that leaving with a stranger is dangerous and won't mind.
- Don't be *too* trusting with people you don't know. A safety-savvy person will not leave her drink unattended at a bar or club and won't accept a drink from someone if she hasn't watched the bartender make it or open the bottle. Both men

- When leaving with a stranger, activate the Find My Friends app (discussed in Chapter 2) on your phone so that a friend or family member can track your location.
- Burners (also discussed in Chapter 2) can be used as a form of protection as well as a form of electronic surveillance. Let's say you're a woman and you meet a man at a bar. You don't know if he's a nice guy, a stalker, or an idiot. You can give him a fake phone number, and if it turns out that he's a good guy and you like him, you can always tell him that you changed your telephone number and give him your real number. If he turns out to be an idiot, you can burn that number, and he won't be able to call you again.

and women can be drugged, robbed, or sexually assaulted.

PEPPER SPRAY

Pepper spray is a useful and nonlethal self-defense weapon. An inflammatory agent, pepper spray, which typically comes in canisters, is a chemical compound that irritates the eyes to cause tears, pain, and temporary blindness. It is often confused with mace, which is an irritant (see chart, page 166). Pepper spray can render an assailant incapacitated for anywhere from fifteen minutes to an hour. The police use it, mail carriers use it, and civilians should carry it, especially women living alone or taking public transportation at night.

It's legal to carry pepper spray as long as you're over the age of eighteen and you purchase it legally. Depending upon where you live (states have varying laws and restrictions on the purchase and possession of pepper spray), you can buy it at a local sporting goods store, drugstore, or gun dealership, or you can purchase it

PEPPER SPRAY VERSUS MACE

Pepper Spray

Classification: Inflammatory agent
Causes: Capillaries to dilate, eyes to shut, coughing, breathing difficulty
Effectiveness: Immediately incapacitates
Legality: Legal for personal use (restrictions may apply)

Mace

Classification: Irritant (similar to tear gas)
Causes: Searing pain, eyes to tear
Effectiveness: Does not work reliably on all individuals
Legality: Illegal for personal use

online. (Obviously, it's not legal to carry pepper spray onto a plane, but you can put it in your luggage. I would recommend putting it in a plastic baggie in case it explodes while you travel.)

It's important that you receive some pepper spray training—rather than just buying it and sticking it in your pocket—because pepper spray can be used against you. There are several rules to effectively using pepper spray:

1. Aim for the chest. Your instinct might be to go for your assailant's head, but the head is a very small target. Rather, aim for the chest, which is a bigger target, and tilt up from there.
2. After you pepper-spray the assailant, get out of there. Run, scream, yell. You don't have to stick around.
3. Pepper spray doesn't belong in the bottom of your purse with the

loose change and packets of gum. Keep it in your coat pocket. Just as a cop puts a gun in his holster to go to work every day, get into the habit of putting your pepper spray into your pocket.

4. Be mindful of the wind! You can actually spray yourself if the air current is blowing in your direction.

5. When you suspect danger, immediately place your hand on the pepper spray. For example, if it's seventy-five degrees outside, and you see a guy wearing a long coat and he's sweating, that's suspicious. *Why is he wearing a coat? Does he have a suicide bomb under there? A shotgun? What's with this guy?* It doesn't make sense, so grab hold of that canister. You're not being paranoid. You're being prepared.

6. If you get pepper-sprayed—either from wind blowback or from an assailant using your weapon against you—rinse your eyes thoroughly with fresh running water. When I was in the police academy and working as a reserve, the higher-ups used to ask the cadets, "Why did you stick that guy's head in the toilet bowl and flush?" The answer? "Hey, he got pepper-sprayed! Plenty of fresh running water!" Cop humor.

PARANOIA VERSUS PREPAREDNESS

Paranoia	Preparedness
"Everybody's out to get me."	"That guy looks suspicious. I'll grab my pepper spray."
"Everything around me is dangerous."	"It's not a good idea to go into this dark alley."
"Oh my God, my food is poisoned!"	"This hot dog doesn't taste right. Let me toss it."
"Why is everyone looking at me?"	"I feel like someone is watching me. Let me play scenarios in my head of *what if*, because I'm not immune to street crime. Nobody is."
Diagnosis: You need to have a mental evaluation.	Diagnosis: You are street-smart and ready for the worst.

I'M NOT A POLICE OFFICER, BUT I PLAY ONE IN REAL LIFE

Anyone and his mother can purchase a police light and stick it on top of a vehicle. There are plenty of clowns who drive around in these old Ford Crown Victorias that they bought from a police auction and who've purchased jackets that read LAPD or NYPD or any other police force. As we discussed in Chapter 7, it is your right to ask for a marked car and a uniformed officer whenever you are approached by a plainclothes cop: *I don't know who you are. I'm not rolling down the window. I'm not turning off my engine until I see a uniformed cop with a marked car.* Additionally:

- If you are approached while your vehicle is stationary, stay inside your vehicle. Once you unlock or open the door, you're vulnerable.
- If you are approached while you are in motion, activate your turn signal and/or flashers and continue driving to a populated area, such as a rest stop or gas station. Sometimes that's enough to scare the imposter away.

DON'T BE A BLING-A-LING

When you advertise, you usually get clients, so always keep your valuables at home or under wraps. Who is a thug going to rob: An upper-middle-class woman who is wearing a diamond ring and an expensive suit or some lady who looks like she's homeless? The nicer you look, the more likely you are to attract all kinds of attention, and cell phones are just as much a target as jewelry, so keep them out of sight.

A friend of mine is a New York City cop. Back in the eighties, he got engaged to a nice Italian girl, and they came to me when I was a diamond dealer to buy a three-carat pear-shaped diamond ring, a real beauty. A few days later, his fiancée was driving in Alphabet City, which, at the time, was not a safe place. She stopped at a stop sign and had her arm out the window, the diamond twinkling in the sunlight. She was on her way to a fitting for her wedding dress and happy as can be. A guy came up to her car window and said, "Give me your ring, or I'll kill you." Bye-bye, ring. Moral of the story? When you put out honey, you're going to get flies.

CONCEALED CARRY

Concealed carry is the practice of carrying a lethal or nonlethal weapon—handgun, Taser, pepper spray—in public in a concealed manner. There is no federal law that addresses the issuance of concealed-carry permits. Concealed-carry laws vary by state, which are labeled as *Shall Issue*, *May Issue*, or *Right Denied*. (For more information, visit usacarry. com/concealed_carry_permit_information. html.) For example, carrying more than two ounces of pepper spray in Florida requires a concealed-carry permit, so it's important to know the legalities of carrying a weapon. Other things to consider:

QUICK TIP

When wearing rings in public, a trick is to turn them around so that the gemstones are hidden against your palm or the inside of your hand.

- If you're not going to train with a weapon, don't get one. You can hurt someone other than the assailant. You can be disarmed. Your weapon can be used against you. Weapon retention is a problem not only for cops, but for civilians too.
- If you're not morally prepared to use a weapon, don't get one.
- When threatened, position yourself so that you are not within striking distance when reaching for a weapon. Maintain that personal space. This way, if someone lunges for it, you have time to react.
- Storage safety is of utmost importance. Keep guns stored unloaded in a safe that is inaccessible to anyone who is not authorized, including children as well as criminals.
- If you don't feel comfortable carrying a weapon, such as a handgun, you can try bluffing your way out of a threatening

situation, as discussed in Chapter 7: "Get away from me, or I'll shoot you. I have a gun." The old finger in the pocket trick. Trust me, it can work.

COMMON HOUSEHOLD ITEMS

When it comes to self-defense, a weapon is not really a weapon until you use it as such, and many common household items can moonlight as weapons when needed.

Keys: An oldie, but goody. If you're walking in a dark area or don't like the surroundings, have your hand in your pocket and your fingers wrapped around your keys. That will give you a tactical advantage. Keys collect good DNA and blood samples, and they don't hurt you, because they're locked into your palm. Trust me, I wouldn't want to be on the receiving end of a punch with a set of keys.

Magazine: Nothing beats *Cosmo*. Roll the magazine up into a cylinder; it's rock hard and like a nightstick. If you're riding the train or bus late at night, buy an issue at a kiosk. If some creep starts to bother you, smash him across the head.

A WORD ABOUT TASERS

A Taser is an electroshock weapon that fires two small electrodes that deliver an electrical current that will disrupt voluntary muscle control and cause neuromuscular incapacitation. Generally speaking, I'm not a fan of Tasers, and I'll tell you why:

- Usually, you only have one shot. That means if you miss the first time, you're in trouble.
- Usually, you have to be within close range, and that cuts down on your reaction time if something goes wrong.

SO LONG, SOCIAL MEDIA

If you suspect you have a stalker, deactivate your social media. All of them—Twitter, Facebook, Pinterest, and the rest—have to go. Many times, people will tell me, "I'll leave them up, and I'll just block him." However, the stalker may have a cousin with whom you're Facebook friends, and he may be able to watch you from his cousin's page. Or he can create a fake identity, posing as a girl from high school, so that you'll accept him as a friend. Better to be safe than sorry.

Handbag: It amazes me how much stuff people cram into their handbags, but all that weight comes in handy. Swing that puppy like you're in an Olympic hammer throw.

Belt: Slip off your belt, and you can use it as a whip. Belts are especially effective if they have a metal buckle.

Umbrellas: I love umbrellas. If you open one up, the assailant can't see you, and you can jam him in the face with it while you kick him in the balls.

SELF-DEFENSE

No normal person wants to fight, but if you're attacked, you need to win and you need to win quickly. Think of self-defense as a tennis match—you don't want to hit volleys for three hours and see who misses. You want to put the ball away—render your assailant incapacitated or injured, and leave quickly. Achieving this can be relatively easy if you know where to strike.

There are various places of vulnerability, or soft targets, on the human body. Use them.

P.I. GLOSSARY

Soft target: a person, place, or thing, such as a part of the body, that is relatively unprotected or vulnerable.

QUICK TIP

If someone grabs you by the wrist and you want to get away, a very effective self-defense move is to yank your hand downward in a sweeping motion as hard as you can; the person's fingers will open up when they reach the end of their grasp. Similarly, if someone is on top of you, grab his wrists, and twist them until his palms are up. This gives him comparatively less strength (if you twisted his palms down, he would have comparatively more strength) and enables you to make a quick move—to attack his soft targets or make a run for it.

Groin: The old tried and true. The groin offers a great target, especially for close encounters when most people are focused on the upper body. Always try to hit low first—*bam* with a knee strike. At the very least, this will cause an assailant to step back, increasing your personal space and reaction time. And if you're grabbed from behind, reach back and go for the testicles. Squeeze and twist!

Throat: In a life-or-death situation, I don't care how big you are, if you're an NFL linebacker or a UFC fighter, you cannot protect your Adam's apple. It only takes about three pounds of pressure to break a trachea, and there's no way to protect that part of the body—you can't do exercises to strengthen it. It's an area that people often forget about. Therefore, if somebody is on top of you and choking you, trying to cut off your air supply, you only have a few seconds before you pass out. Go on the offensive, and punch the assailant in the throat or grab his trachea—you can feel where it is—and try to crush it. It's a very simple move.

Brachial plexus: The brachial plexus is a bundle of nerves that runs down the side of your neck through your shoulders; it controls movement and feeling for arms, forearms, and hands. A strike by

DID YOU KNOW?

Ever notice how the president of the United States, or other dignitaries, shakes hands with constituents? Rather than clasping someone's hand, he will offer only his four fingers (thumb excluded), as if he were handing that person a dead fish. Contrary to popular belief, this is not the sign of a weak handshake. On the contrary, the move signals strength of awareness. It is a self-defense measure. Without interlocking his fingers, the president cannot be grabbed or pulled into a crowd—he can pull right out, if he needs to. (If someone does manage to get a firm hold of the president's hand and doesn't want to let go, the Secret Service will pull the person's thumb up to release the handshake.)

---

the side of your hand, your fist, or your forearm—not even very hard—right at the spot where the neck and shoulder meet can interrupt motor activity and cause temporary dysfunction and near paralysis to that side of the upper body. And, once again, the assailant cannot protect himself against this.

Fingers: Snap the pinky or ring finger. When you break someone's finger, he may lose the will to fight.

Nose: If you're grabbed from behind, throw your head back and head-butt the assailant's nose.

Eyes: If the bad guy can't see, he can't fight. If someone is on top of you or is trying to rape you, gouge out his eyes with your thumbs. Start right in the corners, near his nose, and apply pressure, or just try to pull them out—like you're squeezing a lemon. Do what you need to do to be safe.

SHOOTINGS

Unfortunately, nowadays we have to contend with all kinds of shootings—mall shootings, street shootings, school shootings—

and it is imperative that we learn how to protect ourselves and our children for times of crisis. The best way to keep our families safe is through mental preparation—knowing what to do and what to look for *before* an incident takes place, because once it does, there is often no time to think.

- **Cover.** If you're walking down the street and gunfire erupts—not toward you, but randomly toward others—most people freeze, and then they start running. However, you're not going to outrun a bullet. Instead, you need to find cover, something that will protect you from the gunfire. You need to look for a:
    - Fire hydrant: Although it won't cover you fully, you can squat down and turn sideways, making yourself a smaller target, and you'll have less of a likelihood of getting hit.
    - The engine part of a car: Duck down and huddle beside the front of an automobile, next to the front tire. That bullet isn't going to get through the engine block, and the tire will help protect you from ricocheting bullets. (Do not hide near the trunk end of a car. It's hollow, and a decent-sized-caliber bullet can slice through the thin metal.)
    - Brick wall: Most walls are sheetrock and do not provide cover for a bullet. You want to hide behind a solid brick wall.
    - If you cannot find cover, try to lie as flat on the ground as

PLAY DEAD

Animals do it. So can you. Deception plays an important role in protecting yourself. Any time you can trick or surprise your assailant, do it. For example, if a guy punches you once and you feel like you can't fight back, you're better off lying there and pretending to be unconscious than continuing on. Pretend he gave you that knockout punch, and when he lets his guard down, *bang*, kick him in the groin or punch him with your keys.

you can. Cover your head with your arms. Better to get shot in the arm than in the head.

- **Concealment.** If you can't find cover, you need to look for concealment, something solid to hide behind—a pillar, a staircase, a garbage can, a cardboard refrigerator box. Generally, people won't shoot at what they can't see. There have been noted incidents of cops walking into domestic violence situations that turn sour, and the husband pulls out a gun and aims it at the officer. Instinctively, the officer grabs a plastic bag that's nearby, puts it in front of his face, and ducks out of the room. He is able to do this, because the husband becomes momentarily stymied—he could have easily shot the officer through the bag, but in the heat of the moment, he doesn't realize this and pauses just long enough for the cop to escape.

P.I. GLOSSARY

Concealment: Something—a garbage can, a curtain—that will hide you.

Cover: Something—a brick wall, a fire hydrant, the engine of a car—that will protect you, particularly from gunfire.

EMPOWER CHILDREN

When I was a kid, we had nuclear drills and fire drills. Today, there should be school shooting drills. Unfortunately, when a shooting occurs, many school officials are unprepared. They tell students, "Everybody hide in the closet!" Although hiding in the closet, in the cubbies, wherever you can hide, is great, if we can instead teach our children how to protect themselves using simple techniques, we can undoubtedly increase their likelihood of survival should a shooting incident ever occur.

- If your child is unattended when a shooting occurs, he should know that if he can escape—through an open side door, for example—he should. He should run as quickly as possible away from the source of the gunfire.
- If your child is alone and there is no way to escape, he should—as

STRANGER
DANGER

- Instruct children never to talk to strangers. If they are approached, they should just keep walking or, if need be, running.
- Instruct them never to get close to a car, even if someone is asking for directions or asking for help to find a puppy—a popular scheme. Teach children to maintain their personal space.
- Tell your kids that you would never have someone pick them up unless there has been a prearranged plan. This way, if a stranger approaches your child and says, "Your mother sent me to pick you up," he or she will not go with him. Of course, there are emergencies when you will not be able to pick up your child and will send someone else. For those situations, teach your child a code word—something crazy like *comet* or *banana muffin*—that your replacement can say to your child so that your child knows it's safe to go with that person. Also, remind your children not to tell their friends the code—it should be your little secret.
- Teach your child never to give out personal information—address, phone number, etc.—to unfamiliar people, either in person, over the phone, or on theInternet.
- Teach your children never to tell anyone over the phone that they are home alone. Instead, children should say, "My mom's busy" or "She's not available right now." A criminal will sometimes call to see if you're home before they break in. Children should ask for a phone number, so that you or a guardian can call back. If the person doesn't want to give a number or asks too many questions, it's time to hang up and contact a trusted adult for assistance.

you would—seek cover. He should know to hide behind a brick wall or a large cement staircase.

- If your child is alone, and there is no escape and no cover, he should know to seek concealment—cabinets, closets, anything that will serve to hide him.

- If your child has no time to find cover or concealment, tell him to create his own—turn over tables or desks or whatever he can MacGyver (desks are especially good, because they have layers that reduce the energy of bullets). Tell him to use what is within his reach—a thick textbook or his backpack—and place it in front of him as he backs up toward a door. This will a) protect his vital organs—his core—and b) possibly confuse the shooter, giving your child enough time to make his getaway. If there is no door or way to escape, instruct your child to hold the textbook in front of him and crouch or lie down in a corner of the room in order to make himself as small of a target as he can. This is called *hardening the core*.

The key to protecting yourself is knowledge and practice. That's why police officers go through training—they repeat these countermeasures over and over, because repetition makes them sharp, it makes their training kick in so that they're better able to react. Self-defense needs to be second nature to be most effective. Therefore, when you're out and about, think to yourself: *What would I use for cover? For concealment? Where would I go right now if somebody was following me? Where is the nearest police officer or police station?* Pay attention to what's going on around you. Take precautions. And, most of all, listen to that little voice—that human intuition—inside of you. It knows what it's talking about. ■

10

PRIVATE EYE,

PUBLIC EYE:
HOW TO PROTECT
YOUR FELLOW MAN

In 1998, I worked as an investigator for the bombing of the U.S. embassy in Dar es Salaam, the largest city in Tanzania. For a matter that was captioned "United States of America vs. Usama Bin Laden, et al," I was assigned by the United States District Court, pursuant to the Criminal Justice Act (CJA), during the prosecution of Wadih El-Hage, a former al-Qaeda member. El-Hage, who is currently serving life imprisonment for his part in the bombing, had lived in a suburban community of Arlington, Texas. He had been working in a local tire shop making about minimum wage. He had lived in a small apartment near the University of Texas, and his children had been enrolled in a local Muslim school. And he had been conspiring to murder U.S. nationals and government employees.

And he is not alone.

Today's news is filled with stories like this, stories of people living in American cities, working in American companies, and sending their children to school with American students, who are ready, and planning, to commit terrorism. Their goal is to:

- Assimilate
- Infiltrate
- Activate

It is scary to think that the next terrorist attack can come from a person who is living or working next to you. Public safety is a concern for all of us, whether you live on the crowded streets of a big city or the pebbled roads of a rural town. There are people out there who want to hurt you simply because of who you are, where you live, and what you represent. Every day, members of our government, in conjunction with law enforcement and other agencies, work diligently to stop these criminals and terrorists; however, they cannot be everywhere, which is why they are often

REASONS PEOPLE DON'T GET INVOLVED

- *It's none of my business.* Um, yes, it is.
- *I must be mistaken.* Self-doubt and rational thinking have a way of shutting down our human intuition when we think we see something suspicious. Don't let it!
- *I'm scared if I do something, that person will come after me.* Totally understandable, but there's no need to confront anyone in order to help. Make an anonymous 911 call. Casually approach a police officer. Wouldn't you want someone to help you if you were in trouble?
- *I thought I heard someone scream outside my window last night, but I went back to sleep.* What do you mean you went back to sleep? People are lazy. Get your butt out of bed and go help somebody!
- *Not my problem.* This is probably our biggest hurdle as a nation. Apathy. It is our problem. And it's a big one.

DON'T BE SCARED TO DIAL 911

Law enforcement exists to help us, so you shouldn't be afraid to contact a police officer or the authorities if you see something suspicious.

- You will not be penalized if your suspicions turn out to be easily explained or a misunderstanding. If your call was made in good faith, the authorities will thank you, not arrest you.
- You don't have to give your name. You can call 911 anonymously (block your Caller ID by dialing *67 before you dial) or say you'd rather not be identified.

aided by average and ordinary citizens. Like *you. You* are our eyes and ears on the ground. *You* are our first line of defense against acts of terrorism and crime in general. All of us, together, play a role in keeping our neighborhoods and communities safe. Simply by being alert and keeping your eyes and ears open, you can help nab the bad guys and maybe even save the day. This chapter details private investigation skills that can be used for public good. Read them. Learn them. And use them, if you get the chance. We're counting on you.

IF YOU SEE SOMETHING, SAY SOMETHING

If you see something, say something began as an advertising slogan used by the Metropolitan Transit Authority in New York City in the aftermath of the 9/11 attacks and has since become a global phenomenon. The campaign seeks to raise the public's awareness of terrorism and of violent crime. It carries a simple message: *We're not asking you to be a hero or go out of your way, but if you see something that might affect you and the people around you, don't just keep it to yourself. Tell someone.* As discussed in Chapter 9, all of us have personal threat levels that we use to protect ourselves based upon our circumstances or locations. So too must we have awareness of impending dangers to others, particularly those dangers that are intended to injure a great number of people. It is our duty to be on the lookout for what is considered *suspicious activity* as well as *suspicious objects*.

SUSPICIOUS ACTIVITY

Suspicious activity is any behavior that you observe that you believe to be potentially harmful to you and those around you. Although it can mean different things to different people, suspicious activity refers to behaviors that appear to be out of the ordinary—they stick out during your everyday routine—and make you feel apprehensive or guarded.

Suspicious activity can happen anywhere, but especially in places where large numbers of people assemble, including airports, train stations, bus depots, the epicenters of large cities, college campuses, and elementary, middle, and high schools. The following behaviors should be on your radar; in the past, they have proven to be connected to terrorist activities.

- Tampering with surveillance cameras, whether breaking them, covering them with an object, or blocking them. If you spy anyone doing this who doesn't appear to be a maintenance worker, alert the authorities.
- Leaving a package or piece of luggage alone, such as on a platform or in a parking lot or waiting area. All packages and luggage should be accompanied by a person.
- Parking or abandoning vehicles in odd or heavily populated locations, such as school entrances or transit centers. Ask yourself: *Why did that guy just double-park his truck full of boxes in front of that school, but then walk in the other direction?*
- Driving vehicles without license plates or the proper vehicle tags. This may be to keep from being identified or because the vehicle has been stolen.
- Lingering or loitering, particularly when everyone else seems to be moving around and has somewhere to go. For example, staying

SUSPICIOUS ACTIVITY vs SUSPICIOUS PERSON

Suspicious *activity* does not mean suspicious *person*. Why?

- What a person looks like—ethnicity, race, physical size, religious affiliation—by itself is not suspicious. Rather, it is what that person is doing, where he's going, or what he's carrying that may raise eyebrows.
- Terrorists have gotten smart. They're adapting to American culture. You might be out there looking for people wearing Muslim garb or donning a long beard, but the truth is that today's brand of terrorist is more likely to wear a thousand-dollar suit than a thawb. He is more likely to be eating hot dogs than halal. He has become harder and harder to distinguish, if at all.
- Americans can be terrorists too. Oklahoma City bombing. Boston Marathon bombings. Terrorism has no face. It has many.

for long periods at an airport gate without getting on any flights is suspicious activity.

- Hanging around in concealed locations, such as crawl spaces. Other than for a game of hide and seek, there's absolutely no reason for anyone to be messing around in tight, enclosed spaces in public areas—again, unless he or she is a maintenance worker of some kind and has the credentials to prove it.
- Taking the same public transit routes over and over again without a destination. Terrorists will perform multiple trial runs or timed exercises to make sure their plans run smoothly. This type of behavior is more likely to be noticed by those who work on modes of transportation, such as conductors, but can be picked up by anyone who travels frequently or routinely.
- Entering or breaking into unauthorized areas, particularly in crowded public places, such as airports and train stations. There should be no reason why a transit worker needs to use a crowbar to get into a maintenance room or office.

WHO SHOULD YOU TELL?

Don't take matters into your own hands when you observe suspicious activity and/or objects. It is always best to contact the authorities, who are trained to handle acts of terrorism or other violence against the public. But who exactly is that? It depends on the situation and the circumstances. Here's a quick list:

Location	Who to tell
Public street/park	Police officer, sheriff
On a train	Conductor
On a bus	Bus driver
In a train station	Police officer, transit worker
In an airport	Airport security, police officer
In an office building	Building security, guard
In a hotel	Hotel security, dial 911
At home	Dial 911
If you cannot locate anyone	Dial 911

- Taking an unusual interest in an airport's, train station's, or bus depot's schedule, security, or surveillance equipment/facilities. Be wary of individuals who are counting paces, sketching floor plans, taking notes or measurements, snapping photos, using binoculars or magnifying glasses, or video-recording.
- Appearing fixated on a particular object or building beyond a casual or a professional interest. Terrorists study their locations so that they are prepared to execute their crime.
- Asking too many questions about a building or facility's purpose, operations, personnel, shift changes, and security procedures. Their thirst for knowledge will seem excessive, focusing on the minutest of details.
- Exhibiting the signs of deception we discussed in Chapter 4:
    - Avoiding eye contact and physical contact.
    - Keeping a distance from others.
    - Providing evasive answers or stalling when asked about what they're doing or where they're going.

- Exhibiting unusual or excessive signs of fear. A terrorist might have his eyes open like half dollars because he's got a suicide vest on and he's scared out of his mind.
- Carrying or waving weapons. Don't assume that someone is a police officer, private detective, or any other member of law enforcement.
- Carrying aerosol containers, spray devices, or anything that omits a strange smell or gas. These items can be used for chemical or biological warfare.
- Wearing very loose-fitting or large clothing. Machinery, artillery, aerosol containers—they can all be hidden. Keep in mind that all of us wear overcoats and loose-fitting clothing in cold weather, but terrorists' clothing will appear extremely disproportional to their size.
- Wearing long coats and winter gear, particularly in warm weather. What good reason is there to wear a heavy wool outer garment in the middle of summer? And if the person looks uncomfortable— he is sweating profusely, for example—it is a good indicator that he may be hiding something.
- Transferring or spending an unusually large amount of cash or gift cards at one time. Terrorists need to fund their operations, and they use cash and prepaid credit cards to be untraceable by law enforcement.
- Purchasing large amounts of weapons or bomb-making materials, such as hydrogen peroxide, fuel oil, ammonium nitrate fertilizer, gunpowder, ball bearings, nuts and bolts, or ammunition.
- Purchasing a large amount of one-time-use cell phones. Terrorists use such phones to communicate secretly.
- Stealing uniforms, badges, or credentials, particularly of police, security personnel, or transit workers. For their masquerade, terrorists will take any clothing and/or identifiers they can.

GLOSSARY

Collar:
to arrest or take into custody. *The guy was collared by the police at the airport while he was trying to board a plane.*
Pinched:
arrested. *He got pinched for assaulting a police officer.*

THE DO'S AND DON'TS
OF OBSERVING
SUSPICIOUS ACTIVITY
OR OBJECTS

Do's:

- *Do* observe carefully, so that you can remember as many details as possible.
- *Do* take notes, snap photos, or take brief snippets of videos, if you can, but don't stand there like you are shooting a wedding.
- *Do* notify the authorities as soon as possible.
- *Do* keep your distance from any suspicious activity or object.

Don'ts:

- *Don't* confront the individual. It's not your job, and you don't know what you'll be up against. Your safety can be at risk.
- *Don't* reveal your suspicions to the person doing the suspicious activity or to anyone around you. You can be injured or killed by the suspect. Also, there may be lookouts—average-looking people in the crowd—working with the suspect.
- *Don't* approach, move, or touch any suspicious objects.
- *Don't* alarm anyone—unless you are absolutely, positively sure that something bad is imminent. In other words, if a package is smoking, then, yes, sound the alarm!
- *Don't* take direct action, such as tackling an individual and holding him until the police arrive.
- *Don't* use a cell phone or radio in the immediate vicinity. Radio transmissions can set off explosives, so move away to a safe distance and notify 911.

Upon seeing any suspicious activity, your job, as a citizen, is to alert the authorities. Of course, any or all of the activities listed above may be innocent, but that is up to law enforcement to decide. The authorities will determine whether suspicious behavior warrants further investigation. Just by alerting them, you've done your part. Leave the rest to the professionals.

SUSPICIOUS OBJECTS

In addition to suspicious behaviors, you should be on the lookout for suspicious objects. These may be more difficult to determine, because objects don't usually command our attention in the same ways that people do. As with people, objects in and of themselves may not be problematic; it's the behaviors surrounding them that will be the tip-offs:

- Boxes, bags, or other packages left unattended at busy public transit centers, such as bus depots, train stations, and airports. They may be left on a train track, a platform, or on a seat in a waiting area. They may be partially hidden or in plain sight.
- Boxes, bags, or other packages that are carried onto an airplane or a train or bus and placed in a compartment that is very far away from the traveler, particularly if there is no reason for the great distance (the train is practically empty, for example).
- Large boxes, bags, or other packages that seem to be especially heavy or weigh more than usual.
- Strange smells. Bomb-making materials, such as fuel, heating oil, gasoline, gunpowder, etc., often give off scents.
- Unexplained leaks. If the terrorists are using liquids, the containers in which they're carried may leak.

BUSINESS SMARTS

Business owners must make sure they comply with the provisions of the United States Immigration and Nationalization Act. All employees must have a legal status and the documents to prove it. Most valid forms of identification have holograms and watermarks. Always look closely at paperwork to be sure an applicant hasn't printed and laminated their ID themselves. I've seen it all in my line of work.

- Exposed wiring or other signs of electrical tampering, particularly on airplanes, buses, and trains. Terrorists may splice into the existing wiring of a vehicle for power or the activation of a device.

Again, any of these situations may have a perfectly good explanation—people accidentally leave shopping bags and boxes on modes of transportation all the time. Still, there's no harm in bringing suspicious objects to the attention of the authorities. Better safe than sorry.

A WORD ABOUT NEIGHBORS

I love my neighbors. They're great people. I'm sure yours are too. However, if you see your next-door neighbor dragging large, heavy garbage bags into the trunk of his car early one morning and then read in the newspaper that a teenage girl from your community has gone missing, I don't care how well you think you know your neighbor, if he shovels your walkway in the winter or helps your kids with their math homework, you need to pick up the phone and dial 911.

A friend of mine on Long Island lived next to a family of Middle Eastern descent—*nice people*, she said. Their kids played together. They were chatty, friendly. The day before the attacks of Sept. 11, 2001, my friend was coming home from work, and the father of the family approached her.

"Don't go to Manhattan tomorrow," he said.

"What do you mean?" my friend asked. "I'm not going into Manhattan. I don't have any appointments."

"Oh, good," he said.

She didn't think anything of it. It's strange to think that was the world in which we lived on Sept. 10, 2001—that if someone intimated something bad was imminent, you could just continue with your day as if it never happened. But that's how it was. We all did it. We didn't *know*.

My friend said the father gave the same mild warning to a few other neighbors—that they should stay away from *the City*, as

THE FIVE Ws

We talked briefly in Chapter 5 about how private investigators need to think like journalists when gathering evidence. Journalists use what are called the *Five Ws* when writing a news article to make sure they cover all their bases. You too can use these when reporting suspicious behavior or objects to the authorities:

- **Who:** What did the person who was taking part in the suspicious activity look like? What was the color of his or her skin? Hair? Clothing? How tall was this person?
- **What:** What was this person doing? What was the suspicious activity? What did the suspicious object look like?
- **Where:** Where did the suspicious activity take place? What is the street intersection or the number of the bus or train? Is the activity still taking place? If not, in what direction was the person taking part in the suspicious activity heading? Where did you last see this person? Where did you see the suspicious object? Is it still there?
- **When:** When did you observe the suspicious activity or object? (Ideally, you want to alert the authorities as soon as possible.)
- **Why:** Why did you think this activity or object was suspicious? What was it about this activity or object that caught your eye?

Manhattan is often called by Long Islanders. They, too, thought nothing of it.

Until the next morning.

By the time the first plane hit the World Trade Center, that nice family had already moved out of their home and disappeared. One of the neighbors called the police, and there was a huge crime scene stationed on the block for a month. She told me the officers discovered that the walls of the family's home had been spray-painted with a big *911*.

I don't know what happened to the family, but I do know what happened to all the rest of us. We would never be the same knowing that terrorists could be living among us—or even right next door.

DEPARTMENT OF HOMELAND SECURITY

The U.S. Department of Homeland Security (DHS), established after the 9/11 attacks, handles the primary responsibilities of protecting the United States and its territories from terrorist attacks (as well as man-made accidents and natural disasters). The DHS heads up various agencies that handle our nation's safety, including the Transportation Security Administration (TSA), Coast Guard, and Secret Service, as well as immigration and border security. As a citizen, you can help the DHS perform its duties:

- Border patrol. The United States shares seven thousand miles of land border with Canada and Mexico (as well as rivers, lakes, and coastal waters). The DHS is responsible for protecting our borders from the illegal passage of weapons, drugs, contraband, and people. Most border crossings are in rural areas, places that are not heavily populated. Therefore, criminals often attempt to cross into the country illegally, so they can take part in all sorts of illegal activities. If you live in border towns:
    - Keep an especially keen eye out for suspicious behavior. Individuals who cross over may be looking to commit quick crimes, such as burglaries, robberies, or kidnappings, and then cross back over the border. Also, terrorists may enter into the United States from Mexico and Canada.
    - Keep an especially keen eye out for suspicious objects, such as drugs or guns, which may be smuggled into the country.
    - Keep an especially keen eye out for individuals in distress. Human trafficking is a form of modern-day slavery. It uses force, fraud, and coercion to exploit people for some type of labor or sex purpose, including prostitution, debt bondage, domestic servitude, and farm or factory labor. Victims might be taken against their wishes, or kidnapped, or they may go willingly, lured by people

DID YOU KNOW?

The Minuteman Project is a citizen-run activist organization that was founded in April 2005 to monitor the flow of illegal immigrants along the border between the United States and Mexico. The name is derived from *Minutemen*, the militiamen who fought in the American Revolution.

they trust or strangers with false promises of fame or well-paying jobs. The DHS works with law enforcement, private organizations, and government agencies on a program known as the Blue Campaign, which was created to inform people about the crime of human trafficking and to instruct them about how to report suspected cases. You don't need to possess a very particular set of skills, like Liam Neeson's character in *Taken*, to help combat human trafficking. All you need is observation and the willingness to tell someone if you see something suspicious. It is through working together that we can protect the basic right of freedom.

- Be understanding of the safety precautions being made at checkpoints when traveling out of the country. It is worth a few extra minutes of your time to ensure your safety and that of others.

AMBER ALERTS

Most of us are familiar with the AMBER Alert or child abduction alert system. AMBER, which is an acronym for *America's Missing: Broadcast Emergency Response*, was named for Amber Hagerman, a little girl who was abducted and murdered in Arlington, Texas, in 1996. (Similarly, a SILVER Alert broadcasts information about missing seniors who may have Alzheimer's disease, dementia, or other mental disabilities.) The hours after a child's abduction are critical, and the more people who are out there looking for these children, the more likely they are to be found. Nowadays,

THE MORE YOU KNOW

The best way to be a citizen of your country and of the world is to be an educated one, so it's important to keep current on news events:

- Read newspapers and watch or listen to local and international newscasts regularly.
- Get your news from objective sources, not only from your Uncle Bud at the dinner table or Jimmy Fallon while you're lying in bed.
- Get your news from various sources, beyond the networks with which you align politically. Switch it up every now and then to see what others have to say.

wireless technology is helping to galvanize communities to assist law enforcement in the search for and return of abducted children. You may opt in to receive alerts on your wireless devices by visiting missingkids.com/ambersignup/.

Tips to keep in mind regarding child predators:

- Any adult can be a child abductor, child abuser, or pedophile. Again, it can be your neighbor, your boss, your business associate, or someone in your own family. Most child molesters are known to the children they abuse.
- Child abusers have common behaviors:
  - They tend to talk about or treat children as if they were adults.
  - They tend to say they love all children and are very childlike.
  - They look for vulnerable children, particularly those who do not have a strong family network of support.
- As mentioned in Chapter 7, visit the U.S. Department of Justice's National Sex Offender Database (nsopw.gov/en-US) to determine whether any registered sex offenders live near your home. You can enter your zip code and do a general search, or you can also plug in individual names to see if a specific person is a sex offender.

WORKING TOGETHER

After 9/11, I was a busy guy. I worked with building managements and staff to create evacuation procedures in the event of terrorist acts. I also worked with school administrators to assess and implement plans regarding active shooters. This included giving recommendations for the fortification of their schools' electronic and security protocols—buzzers, television cameras, access codes—and instructing on how to fortify sections of walls with cinder block (rather than sheetrock) to make them bulletproof, so that the students knew where to hide and what to do as a unit.

However, as the years have passed, and as our government and law enforcement agencies continue to thwart terrorist activity, people's attention to safety tends to become lax. There's always an ebb and flow: When something horrific happens, we all clamor for tightened precautions and systems, but the longer the time is between incidents, the more we, as a nation, grow forgetful or are lulled into a false sense of security.

We need to be ever vigilant. Law enforcement works diligently on our behalf every day, but police officers are primarily a reactive force—they act in response to an event. True public safety relies on an army of private citizens—millions of people protecting their communities by keeping their eyes open and reporting suspicious activity immediately and without hesitation.

Resilience with regard to public safety and acts of terrorism is the shared responsibility of us all—government, law enforcement, the private and nonprofit sectors, and individual citizens. The more we good guys can work together and look out for one another, the safer our world will be. So if you see something, say something. Today. Tomorrow. Always. █

11

WHAT WOULD DAN DO?

So what do you think? Are you ready to take a crack at private investigation? Are you ready to go into the field? Find old friends? Take on the liars and the scammers? Let's see what you've got! What follows are fifteen real-life scenarios—some are taken straight from my years as a private investigator in New York City, while others are similar to jobs I've done. Examine each situation, form a plan of action, and then compare your strategy to mine.

1
You suspect your child is using drugs. How would you go about finding out?

WHAT WOULD DAN DO?

I would search my child's room, backpack, and any suspected hiding places where drugs might be concealed in the house. Then I would speak to my child, utilizing the forensic interview techniques specified in Chapter 4, to see if he or she is being truthful. If any evidence of drugs or paraphernalia were found during the search, I would present that to my child as part of the interview. Then I'd also ask my child to take a urinalysis drug test, which I purchased at a pharmacy or online.

2
You meet someone at a bar whom you think is nice and want to give that person your phone number. How would you decide?

WHAT WOULD DAN DO?

As discussed in Chapter 9, I would provide the stranger with a burner number. This way, if this person turns out to be a creep or a psycho, my real number is not known.

3
You are walking down the street and sense your ex has somebody watching you, probably to see if you're dating someone else. You keep seeing the same person in various places that you go. What should you do?

WHAT WOULD DAN DO?

Using the counter-surveillance techniques detailed in Chapter 9, I would stop walking and pretend to look into a store window. Utilizing the reflection of the window, I could see if that person has stopped too and is hovering around me. Then I would switch directions and walk the opposite way. I would cross the street and confirm whether or not the person was, in fact, following me. If the answer is yes, I would enter a safe location, such as a store, restaurant, or other public place, and call the police or ask a store employee to contact the police for me.

 You are concerned that your wife is having an affair. What should you do?

WHAT WOULD DAN DO?

I would utilize the tactics detailed in Chapters 1 and 2 in order to witness firsthand the activities of the suspected philanderer or those detailed in Chapter 5 to obtain evidence of those activities:

- If I had legal access to my wife's phone records, I would check for repeated numbers that were called at times when I wasn't home, or for numbers with repeated back-and-forth texts.
- I might check the undergarments of my wife after she places them in the hamper. Utilizing commercially available test kits, I would check for the presence of semen. If the undergarments tested positive, I would send them to a DNA laboratory along with my DNA sample to see if the semen matched.

 You're leaving work to have dinner with friends. You have to bring files and your laptop home, because you are leaving for a business trip the following day. You don't want to carry your briefcase all during dinner. It's a pain in the neck. You would rather leave your stuff in the car, hidden under a seat or in the trunk. After all, that's why you paid more for tinted windows and a state-of-the-art alarm system. What should you do?

WHAT WOULD DAN DO?

I would never leave any work-related files or valuable electronics containing sensitive information in my vehicle. Vehicles are very easy to break into. Even with a state-of-the-art alarm system, all it takes is a second for a thief to smash the window or pop the trunk open and run off with your stuff as the alarm wakes up the entire neighborhood. And hiding your stuff doesn't do much good either if the thief has been tailing you or is watching your every move. Don't be lazy. Carry your briefcase with you. Keep it between your legs under the table during dinner. Don't check it with the coat-check person.

 You are walking to your car after getting off the train. It is late at night, and no one else got off at the same stop. As you walk toward your car, someone grabs you from behind and puts you in a chokehold. What should you do?

WHAT WOULD DAN DO?

As soon as I got off the train, I would be on guard for potential danger. Any time you are walking alone at night or through some place that is creepy, you should instantly raise your personal threat level, as discussed in Chapter 9. I would place my keys in the palm of my hand, with the individual keys protruding between my fingers. When I am grabbed from behind, I would punch the face and head of the assailant as hard as I could. Remember, when you are being choked, you only have seconds before you pass out from the loss of blood flow or oxygen to your brain. Drastic measures need to be taken immediately!

 You have a petty cash box in your drawer at work. You notice that money has been stolen periodically, and you don't have security cameras installed in your office. What should you do?

WHAT WOULD DAN DO?

I would carry on, business as usual, and not mention anything to any of my employees. As detailed in Chapter 5, I would purchase fluorescent powder and an ultraviolet black light. I would dust the box and the money with the powder. When another theft was detected, I would use the black light to look at my employees' hands as well as their keys, work areas, pens, and computer keyboards for transference of the powder, since the items would be glowing. After firing the culprit and possibly having him arrested for theft, I would transfer the petty cash to a locked drawer and then go out and buy a safe and a recording camera to install in my office so this type of thing doesn't happen again.

8 **You think your employees are goofing off while you are out of the office. What should you do?**

WHAT WOULD DAN DO?

I would install some surveillance cameras as detailed in Chapter 2. This way, I can monitor my employees' activities from my computer, tablet, or smartphone. They will be less likely to goof off if they know the boss is watching.

 You are thinking of hiring a contractor you've seen doing some work in the neighborhood to fix the front porch of your house, but you're not sure if that person is reputable. What should you do?

WHAT WOULD DAN DO?

I would follow the screening process detailed in Chapter 7. I would knock on the doors of my neighbors who utilized the contractor's services to see if they were satisfied with his work and working relationship, and ask if they would recommend him. I would visit my local government agency to see if there are any outstanding complaints or pending legal issues associated with the guy. Then I would conduct a background check on him to see if anything else turned up. Once I think the guy is okay, I will hire him, but still continue to watch him closely for signs of deception, as discussed in Chapter 4.

10 You mistakenly clicked on a link that came in an unsolicited e-mail, and now you think that you have a virus or malware installed on your computer. What should you do?

WHAT WOULD DAN DO?

After kicking myself, I would run a thorough scan of my computer using any well-known, high-quality virus protection program. (I would pay for it and not use the free versions. The paid versions have many features that the free versions do not have.) If a virus is found and not cured, I would call my computer's tech support for assistance with the virus removal. If that doesn't help, I would take the computer to a reputable computer tech and have him fix the problem.

11 Someone is knocking at your door, and you're not expecting anyone, but you saw your neighbor's daughter outside your window earlier, and she was selling Girl Scout cookies. You think it's probably her. What should you do?

WHAT WOULD DAN DO?

I would never open the door if I am not expecting a visitor, no matter whom I saw walking around my block or neighborhood. Burglars and home invaders carefully choose the homes they violate. What better time to hit a house than when there are trick-or-treaters present or young girls selling cookies? As discussed in Chapter 7, I would ask through the door what the visitor wants. If it is a salesman or company representative, I would ask him to leave ID, so that I can validate his claims at a later date if I am interested in his offer. If it is my neighbor and her daughter, who I would recognize by looking through my door's peephole, I would open the door and buy a box of Samoas.

12 You are getting serious with a guy you're dating. However, things about him are sketchy. You're not sure if he is being truthful with you about his past. What should you do?

WHAT WOULD DAN DO?

I would make a list of the things that don't add up and conduct a background check as detailed in Chapter 5—searching for a criminal past, lawsuits, judgments, liens, and bankruptcies, at a minimum. There are many scammers who prey on nice people. Don't let love blind you. Do your homework!

13 You are going through a divorce and don't want your spouse getting access to your credit card accounts, bank accounts, e-mails, or cell phone records. What should you do to protect yourself?

WHAT WOULD DAN DO?

I would password-protect all my accounts with passwords that my spouse couldn't figure out. As detailed in Chapter 8, I would make up a password that is complex and does not relate to things I like—for example, if I'm a Mets fan, I wouldn't use *No1MetFan56* as my password.

14 You don't trust your boyfriend, and it is driving you crazy. You want to put a GPS device on his car so you know where he is at all times. Should you?

WHAT WOULD DAN DO?

I would never put a GPS tracking advice on a car that is not owned by me. In most states, you must be the owner of the vehicle to put a GPS tracking device on it, and in some states it may not be legal without the consent of the driver, regardless of whether or not you own the car. I would check with an attorney to make sure. Otherwise, I could be facing felony charges. Instead, I would try conducting a moving surveillance to monitor his whereabouts.

15 You are following your girlfriend around to see if she is cheating on you. She was able to get through the red light before it changed. What should you do? Should you wait until traffic clears, or run the red light and speed up to catch her?

WHAT WOULD DAN DO?

As I mention in Chapter 1, I would not break any laws, including speed limit laws, to pursue someone. I could be charged with reckless endangerment or negligent homicide if someone gets killed. I would go home and try again another day.

How did you do? Every day is an adventure in private investigation. Remember to always think smart, keep your cool, and, most importantly, be safe! With training and practice, you can learn to track people, question subjects, and gather research like a pro. Who knows? Maybe one day, I'll even learn a little something from you!

ACKNOWLEDGMENTS

This book would not be possible without the support and guidance of many people in my life:

My wife, Barbara, for being by my side since we were fifteen years old. You are my inspiration to succeed.

My three children—Lance, Lisa, and Richard—who have helped me build my business from scratch.

My brother, Elie, and sister, Raquel, who have assisted me in many ways throughout my career.

Writer and editor Dina Santorelli for all your hard work and enthusiasm for this book.

Marc Resnick, executive editor of St. Martin's Press, and Steve Cohen, executive vice president and chief operating officer of Macmillan Publishers, for making a dream of mine come true.

Ellen Scordato and the rest of the Stonesong team for helping to turn this book from an idea to a reality.

My staff at International Investigative Group, Ltd., because no man is an island.

Nathan Gordon and William Fletcher from the Academy of Scientific Training for your insight, research, teaching, and mentoring.

Harley, my maltipoo, for being the best friend a man could ever have.

And, finally, to the men and women of our Reserve and Auxiliary police forces in New York and throughout the United States for your inspiration, your sense of duty, and your selfless dedication to our communities.

RESOURCES

Want more? Here's a list of associations, organizations, Web sites, and government resources to help you further your journey of private investigation. Good luck!

ALUMNI
- AlumniClass: http://www.alumniclass.com
- Alumz: http://www.alumz.com
- Classmates.com: http://www.classmates.com
- Reunion.com: http://www.reunion.com

ASSOCIATIONS/SOCIETIES/REGISTRIES
- National Do Not Call Registry: http://www.donotcall.gov
- The Vidocq Society: http://www.vidocq.org

BACKGROUND CHECKS/SCREENINGS/VETTING/ REVIEWS
- Angie's List: http://www.angieslist.com
- DNA Diagnostic Center: http://www.dnacenter.com
- MedlinePlus (semen analysis): http://www.nlm.nih.gov/ medlineplus/ency/article/003627.htm
- Yelp: http://www.yelp.com

CREDIBILITY ASSESSMENT
- Center for Nonverbal Studies: http://center-for-nonverbal-studies.org
- National Center for Credibility Assessment: http://www.ncca.mil

CREDIT REPORTING COMPANIES
- Equifax: http://www.equifax.com, (800) 525-6285
- Experian: http://www.experian.com, (888) 397-3742
- TransUnion: http://www.transunion.com, (800) 680-7289

CRIME DATA
- http://city-data.com
- http://neighborhoodscout.com

DAN RIBACOFF
- Facebook: https://www.facebook.com/DanielRibacoffPI
- Instagram: https://instagram.com/danielribacoff
- International Investigative Group, Ltd. (my company): http://iigpi.com
- *The Steve Wilkos Show*: http://www.stevewilkos.com/our_team/daniel-ribacoff
- Twitter: http://twitter.com/danielribacoff

DATA PROTECTION
- Keeper (passwords): http://keepersecurity.com
- LifeLock: http://www.lifelock.com

DIRECTORIES
- 411.com: http://www.411.com
- Anywho: http://www.anywho.com
- Federal Bureau of Prisons (inmate locator): http://www.bop.gov/inmateloc
- Financial Industry Regulatory Authority (investment advisors): http://www.finra.org
- Google Alerts: http://google.com/alerts
- Intelius: http://www.intelius.com
- MyLife: http://www.peoplefinders.com
- PeekYou: http://www.peekyou.com
- PeepLo: http://www.peeplo.com
- People Smart: http://www.peoplesmart.com
- PeopleFinders: http://www.peoplefinders.com
- Pipl: http://www.pipl.com
- Radaris: http://radaris.com
- Skipease: http://www.skipease.com
- Spokeo: http://www.spokeo.com
- Switchboard: http://www.switchboard.com
- USNPL: http://www.usnpl.com

- White Pages: http://www.whitepages.com
- Zabasearch: http://www.zabasearch.com

E-MAIL TRACKING SERVICES
- ReadNotify: https://www.readnotify.com

ENTRAPMENT
- Foundation for Economic Education (entrapment): http://fee.org/freeman/detail/law-enforcement-by-deceit-entrapment-and-due-process

FILE/DOCUMENT STORAGE
- Carbonite: http://www.carbonite.com
- Dropbox: http://www.dropbox.com
- Mozy: http://www.mozy.com

FORENSIC PRODUCTS/SUPPLIES
- Sirchie: http://www.sirchie.com

GENEALOGY
- Ancestry: http://www.ancestry.com
- Archives: http://www.archives.com
- CensusRecords.com: https://www.censusrecords.com
- FamilySearch: https://www.familysearch.org
- Find a Grave: http://www.findagrave.com
- Genealogy.com: http://www.genealogy.com
- GenealogyBank.com: http://www.genealogybank.com
- Geni.com: http://www.geni.com
- HeritageQuest.com: http://www.heritagequestonline.com
- MyHeritage.com: http://www.myheritage.com
- The USGenWeb Project: http://www.usgenweb.org
- U.S. Citizenship and Immigration Services: http://www.uscis.gov/genealogy

GUN LAWS

- Law Center to Prevent Gun Violence (search gun laws by state): http://smartgunlaws.org/search-gun-law-by-state
- USA Carry (concealed carry permit information by state): http://www.usacarry.com/concealed_carry_permit_information.html

IDENTITY THEFT/FRAUD/SCAMS

- Department of Justice: http://www.justice.gov/criminal/fraud/websites/idtheft.html
- Federal Bureau of Investigation (common fraud schemes): http://www.fbi.gov/scams-safety
- Federal Trade Commission: http://www.consumer.ftc.gov/features/feature-0014-identity-theft

MAPS/NAVIGATION

- E-ZPass (New York Service Center): https://www.e-zpassny.com/en/home/index.shtml
- GPS.gov: http://www.gps.gov
- Google Earth: https://www.google.com/earth
- Google Maps: http://www.google.com/maps
- Mapquest: http://www.mapquest.com
- MetroCard: http://web.mta.info/metrocard

MISSING CHILDREN/RUNAWAYS

- AMBER Alert:
  http://www.amberalert.gov
  http://www.missingkids.com
- AMBER Alert signup:
  http://www.missingkids.com/ambersignup
  http://www.wirelessamberalerts.org
- National Center for Missing & Exploited Children: http://www.missingkids.com/home
- National Runaway Safeline: http://www.1800runaway.org

MOBILE PAYMENT SOFTWARE

- Apple Pay: https://www.apple.com/apple-pay
- Google Wallet: https://www.google.com/wallet

ONLINE DATING

- AARP: http://dating.aarp.org
- Ashley Madison: http://www.ashleymadison.com
- AYI: http://www.ayi.com
- BeautifulPeople.com: http://www.beautifulpeople.com
- Chemistry.com: http://www.chemistry.com
- Christian Mingle: http://www.christianmingle.com
- Coffee Meets Bagel: http://www.coffeemeetsbagel.com
- Cupid.com: http://www.cupid.com
- Date Hookup: http://www.datehookup.com
- eHarmony: http://www.eharmony.com
- EligibleGreeks: http://www.eligiblegreeks.com
- eVow: http://www.evow.com
- FarmersOnly.com: http://www.farmersonly.com
- JDate (for Jewish singles): http://www.jdate.com
- Match: http://www.match.com
- Matchmaker.com: http://www.matchmaker.com
- Mate1.com: http://www.mate1.com
- Meetup: http://www.meetup.com
- Meet Me: http://home.meetme.com
- Mingle2: http://www.mingle2.com
- OkCupid: http://www.okcupid.com
- PerfectMatch: http://www.perfectmatch.com
- Plenty of Fish: http://www.pof.com
- OurTime.com: http://www.ourtime.com
- Skout: http://www.skout.com
- Spark.com: http://www.spark.com
- SpeedDate: http://www.speeddate.com
- Tinder: http://www.gotinder.com
- Zoosk: https://www.zoosk.com

ONLINE SHOPPING

- National Cyber Security Alliance: https://www.staysafeonline.org/stay-safe-online/protect-your-personal-information/online-shopping

ORDERS OF PROTECTION/RESTRAINING ORDERS

- Family Violence Law Center:
  http://fvlc.org/learn/know-the-law/restraining-orders
- New York State Unified Court System:
  http://www.nycourts.gov/faq/orderofprotection.shtml
- WomensLaw.org: http://www.womenslaw.org/
  laws_state_type.php?id=561&state_code=NY

PEER-TO-PEER FILE SHARING

- Federal Trade Commission: http://www.ftc.gov/tips-advice/
  business-center/guidance/peer-peer-file-sharing-guide-business

PUBLIC RECORDS

- ACRIS (NYC real property records): http://a836-acris.nyc.gov/CP/
- CanIVote.org (registered voter info): http://www.canivote.org
- Census data: http://census.gov
- Instant Checkmate: http://www.instantcheckmate.com
- National Archives (census public records)
  http://www.archives.gov/research/census
- National Center for State Courts: http://ncsc.org
- PACER (court electronic records): https://www.pacer.gov
- RECAP The Law (used in conjunction with PACER):
  https://www.recapthelaw.org
- Search Systems (public records): http://www.searchsystems.net
- United States Courts: http://www.uscourts.gov/CourtRecords.aspx
- VINELink (National Victim Notification Network):
  http://www.vinelink.com

PUBLIC SAFETY

- Blue Campaign (human trafficking): bluecampaign@hq.dhs.gov
- Consumer Product Safety Commission (smoke, carbon monoxide
  detector info): http://www.cpsc.gov
- Department of Homeland Security (human trafficking):
  1-866-347-2423 (toll free)
  1-802-872-6199 (non-toll free international)
- Department of Homeland Security (if you see something, say
  something): http://www.dhs.gov/see-something-say-something

- Environmental Protection Agency (Superfund sites): http://www.epa.gov/superfund/sites
- National Human Trafficking Resource Center (NHTRC): 1-888-373-7888
- New York City: 1-888-NYC-SAFE
- SecureTransit.org: http://www.securetransit.org
- U.S. Immigration and Customs Enforcement (human trafficking): http://www.ice.gov/webform/hsi-tip-form
- U.S. Citizenship and Immigration Services (e-verify): http://www.uscis.gov/e-verify

REGISTERED SEX OFFENDERS
- Dru Sjodin National Sex Offender Public Website (NSOPW): http://www.nsopw.gov/en
- Family Watchdog: http://www.familywatchdog.us
- National Sex Offender Registry: http://www.nationalsexoffenderregistry.com
- NSOPW: http://www.nsopw.gov

SEARCH ENGINES
- Ask: http://ask.com
- Bing: http://bing.com
- Google: http://google.com
- Yahoo: http://yahoo.com

SECURITY LIGHTING
- Security Lighting Systems (commercial): http://www.securitylighting.com
- TCP Lighting: http://www.tcpi.com

SOCIAL NETWORKING

- Blogger: http://www.blogger.com
- Facebook: http://www.facebook.com
- Flickr: http://www.flickr.com
- Foursquare: http://www.foursquare.com
- Goodreads: http://www.goodreads.com
- Google+: http://plus.google.com
- Instagram: http://www.instagram.com
- LinkedIn: http://www.linkedin.com
- Pinterest: http://www.pinterest.com
- Tumblr: http://www.tumblr.com
- Twitter: http://www.twitter.com
- Wattpad: http://www.wattpad.com/signup
- Wordpress: http://www.wordpress.com
- YouTube: http://www.youtube.com

SPOOFING/PHISHING/CALLER ID

- Federal Communications Commission (FCC):
  http://www.fcc.gov/guides/caller-id-and-spoofing
- Federal Trade Commission (FTC):
  http://www.consumer.ftc.gov/articles/0003-phishing

STALKING/HARASSMENT

- National Association for Victim Assistance (harassment/stalking):
  http://www.trynova.org/crime-victim/specializations/harassment-stalking
- National Conference of State Legislatures:
  http://www.ncsl.org/research/telecommunications-and-information-technology/cyberstalking-and-cyberharassment-laws.aspx
- Privacy Rights Clearinghouse:
  https://www.privacyrights.org/are-you-being-stalked
- Stalking Resource Center:
  http://www.victimsofcrime.org/our-programs/stalking-resource-center/stalking-laws/federal-stalking-laws

WANTED PERSONS/MISSING PERSONS

- Federal Bureau of Investigations: http://www.fbi.gov/wanted
- Interpol (wanted persons): http://www.interpol.int/notice/search/wanted
- Interpol (missing persons): http://www.interpol.int/notice/search/missing
- USA.gov (America's most wanted criminals): http://www.usa.gov/Citizen/Topics/MostWanted.shtml

WEB SITE LOCATOR

- DOMAINTOOLS: http://www.domaintools.com
- Internet Archive: http://www.archive.org

FURTHER READING

Bassett, James W. *Solving Employee Theft: New Insights, New Tactics.* BookSurge Publishing, 2008.

Birzer, Michael L. and Cliff Roberson. *Introduction to Criminal Investigation.* Boca Raton, FL: CRC Press, 2011.

Christensen, Loren W. and Lisa Place. *Fight Back: A Woman's Guide to Self-Defense that Works.* Santa Fe, NM: Turtle Press, 2011.

Gordon, Nate. *Nonverbal Behavior in the Martial Arts.* CreateSpace Independent Publishing, 2014.

Houston, Philip, Mike Floyd and Susan Carnicero. *Spy The Lie: Former CIA Officers Teach You How To Detect Deception.* New York: St. Martin's Griffin, 2013.

McClish, Mark. *I Know You Are Lying: Detecting Deception through Statement Analysis.* Harrisburg, PA: Marpa Group, 2001.

Morrison, James and Thomas Anders. *Interviewing Children and Adolescents.* New York: Guilford Press, 2001.

Navarro, Joe and Marvin Karlins. *What Every Body Is Saying: An Ex-FBI Agent's Guide to Speed-Reading People.* New York: William Morrow, 2008.

Pedneault, Stephen. *Preventing and Detecting Employee Theft and Embezzlement: A Practical Guide.* Hoboken: John Wiley & Sons., 2010.

Polson, Beth and Miller Newton, Ph.D. *Not My Kid: A Parent's Guide to Kids and Drugs.* New York: Avon Books, 1986.

Volonino, Linda and Reynaldo Anzaldua. *Computer Forensics for Dummies.* Hoboken: For Dummies, 2008.

Wilson, J. Clare and Martine Powell. *A Guide for Interviewing Children: Essential Skills for Counsellors, Police, Lawyers and Social Workers.* New York: Routledge, 2001.

INDEX

A

Activity, suspicious, 182–187, 196–197
Alarm systems, 128, 129
Aliases, most common, 115
Alumni websites, 45, 204
AMBER Alerts, 191–192
Appearance, changing, 113, 160–162
Asset (informant), 51
Assets, locating, 98–100
ATM information theft, 144–146
Audio surveillance, 26–27, 29
Awareness, level of, 156–159

B

Background checks, 48, 100–104, 201
Behaviors, suspicious, 182–189
Belt, as weapon, 171
Bicycles, for moving surveillance, 21–22
Birdwhistell, Ray, 66
Blogs, 44
Body language, 65–69
Border crossings, 190–191
Burglaries, 122–125, 127
Burners, 33–34, 165
Business owners
  employee theft, 198–199
  hiring provisions for, 187
  investigating employee slacking, 199
  monitoring employee computer use, 30–31
  preventing identity or information theft, 152
  protecting business location and valuables (See Location security)

C

Caller ID, 32–33, 35, 181, 206
Caller ID spoofing, 32

Cameras. See Security cameras; Video surveillance
Cars, for moving surveillance, 18–20
Case (definition), 120
Cell phone monitoring, 32, 34
Cheating spouses
  interrogating, 73
  investigating, 197
  signs of, 57
Children
  AMBER Alerts, 191–192
  child predators, 192
  destinations of runaway teens, 38
  resources for missing children/runaways, 206
  safety during school shootings, 175–177
  stranger danger tips, 176
  suspected drug use by, 73, 196
Circumstantial evidence, 81
Collar (definition), 185
Company websites, 111
Computer surveillance (monitoring) software, 146
Computer viruses, 200
Concealed carry, 169–170
Concealment
  during shootings, 175
  during stakeouts, 13–14
Confessions
  false, 59
  impending, signs of, 69, 71–73
Confidentiality issues, with spyware, 31
Conflict of interest, xv
Contractors, investigating, 126, 199
Court records, 46–47
Cover, during shootings, 174–175
Credibility assessment, 56, 203. See also Lie detection
Credit cards, 152–153
  theft of, 143 (See also Identity theft)
  virtual, 153
  and virtual disappearance, 111

Credit reporting companies, 150, 203
Crimes. *See also* Felony offenses
  data resources on, 204
  using burners, 33–34
Criminal records, 47–49

D

Data protection resources, 204
Date of birth (DOB), 45
Debit cards, 152
Deception burglary, 123
Delayed responses, deception and, 61–62
Direct evidence, 79–81
Directories, online, 44–45, 205–206
Directory assistance, 50
Disappearing. *See* Virtually disappearing
Disguises, 160–162
Distance, for stakeouts, 12
Distraction burglary, 123
Diverting blame, 63
Divorce, 52, 201
DNA testing, 95–97
DOB (date of birth), 45
Document storage, 206
Domestic Violence Hotline, 107
Doormen
  as informants, 51, 85–88
  as security, 109, 110
Doors
  for location security, 132–133
  matchstick trick for monitoring, 129
  precautions when opening, 120–122, 200
Drones, 16–17
Drug testing, 92
Drug use, suspected, 73, 196
Due diligence, 98
Dumpster diving, 82–84, 140–141

E

Eavesdropping, 25
800 numbers, 35–36
Electronic surveillance, 23–36
  audio, 26–27, 29
  burners, 33–34

caller ID, 32–33
  cell phone monitoring, 32
  defined, 24
  felony offenses related to, 29
  identifying private numbers, 34–36
  ownership of devices, 25, 26
  permission for, 25
  reasons for using, 24
  spyware, 30–31
  untraceable phones, 34
  video, 27–30
El-Hage, Wadih, 179
Email
  fraudulent, 147–149
  tracking services for, 206
Email addresses, 108–109
Employee computer monitoring, 30–31
Employee slacking, 199
Employee theft, 198–199
Employment, virtual disappearance and, 112
Entrapment, 206
Environment
  being aware of, 158
  stakeouts and differences in, 15–16
Evasion, 60, 61
Evidence, 79–80
  circumstantial, 81
  direct, 79–81
Evidence gathering, 79–104
  background checks, 100–104
  DNA testing, 95–97
  drug testing, 92
  fingerprint analysis, 92–95
  Five Ws in, 189
  from garbage, 82–84
  from informants, 84–92
  locating assets, 98–100
  online, 96–98
  physical evidence, 81–84
  in serious matters, 89
E-ZPass, 18, 34, 82, 113

F

Facebook, 41
Facial expression, 65

Family
  as informants, 88–90
  safety of (*See* Location security)
Felony offenses
  with electronic surveillance, 29
  with virtually disappearing, 113
File storage, 206
Financial identity theft, 139
Finding people, 37–54
  with GPS, 50–51
  identifiers in, 39
  offline resources for, 49–54
  with online directories, 44–45
  online resources for, 39–49
  with patterns and profiling, 53–54
  with professional websites, 42–44
  resources for, 207, 212
  with search engines, 40
  by setting traps, 53
  with social media, 40–42
  through directory assistance, 50
  through informants, 51–53
  through public records, 45–49
  and top destinations of runaway
    teens, 38
Find My Friends, 25, 165
Fingerprints, 92–95, 113
Five Ws, 189
Fixed surveillance. *See* Stationary
  surveillance
Following someone
  breaking laws when, 202
  when you think you're being
    followed, 196–197
Foot, surveillance on, 20–21
Forensic products/supplies, 206

G

Garbage retrieval, 82–84, 140–141
Genealogy websites, 45, 205
Going off-grid, 114–116
Goodreads, 42
Google, 33
Google Alerts, 98
Google Earth, 98
GPS technologies, finding people
  with, 50–51

GPS tracking devices, 29, 161–162,
  201–202

H

Habits, changing, 113
Hagerman, Amber, 191
Handbag, as weapon, 171
Handheld lie detectors, 75
Handshakes, 173
Harassment resources, 210
Hardening the target (definition), 132
Hidden assets, 100
Home invasions, 118, 120–122
Home security. *See* Location security
Honestly, guilty person's use of, 63
Human trafficking, 190, 191

I

Identifiers, 39
Identity theft, 139–153, 207
  ATM skimmers and keypads,
    145–146
  dumpster diving, 140–141
  kinds of, 139–140
  mail scams, 142
  mail theft, 143
  monitoring (computer surveillance)
    software, 146
  online shopping, 152–153
  passwords, 150–152
  peer-to-peer file sharing, 146–147
  phishing, 147–149
  responding to, 150
  shoulder surfing, 142, 144
  spoofing, 148
  thwarting pickpockets, 144
  vishing (voice phishing), 149
Income tax fraud, 140
Indoor lighting, 132
Informants, 84–92
  doormen and service workers,
    85–88
  family as, 88–90
  finding people through, 51–53
  neighbors as, 90–92
  taking statements from, 87
  tips for using, 84
Insurance, 134–135

Insurance identity theft, 140
Interrogations, 56
  do's and dont's for, 73
  false confessions from, 59
  lie detection in, 56, 58–60
  signs of impending confessions in,
    69, 71–73
Interviews, 56–58
Invasion of privacy, 25

K

Keylogging software, 146
Keys, as weapon, 170
Kinesics, 66

L

Licensing, xi
Lie detection, 55–78
  body language in, 65–69
  with interviews and interrogations,
    56–60
  with polygraphs, 74–78
  signs of impending confessions,
    69, 71–73
  subconscious strategies used to
    deceive, 60–65
  in written communications, 70
Lighting, for location security,
  130–132, 210
Linguistic Statement Analysis
  Techniques (LSAT), 70
LinkedIn, 41
Locating people. *See* Finding
  people
Location security, 117–138
  alarm systems, 128, 129
  assessing new neighborhoods for,
    119
  burglaries, 122–125
  common-sense tips for, 134–135
  constant vigilance for, 125–127
  doors and locks, 132–133
  home invasions, 118, 120–122
  lighting, 130–132
  for offsite events, 125
  safety devices for, 131
  security cameras, 128–130
  weapons, 133, 134

Locks, 132–133
LSAT (Linguistic Statement Analysis
  Techniques), 70
Lying to police officers, 11

M

Mace, 166
Madoff, Bernie, 104
Magazines, as weapons, 170
Mail drop, 109
Mail scams, 142
Mail theft, 143
Malware, computer, 146, 200
Map resources, 207
Medical identity theft, 140
Miller Brewing, 32
Minuteman Project, 191
Missing persons
  AMBER Alerts, 191–192
  resources for finding, 207, 212
  runaways, 38, 207
Mobile payment software, 153, 207
Monitoring software, 146
Moving (rolling) surveillance, 17–22
  on a bicycle, 21–22
  in a car, 18–20
  essentials for, 18
  on foot, 20–21
  practicing, 22

N

Name change, for virtual
  disappearance, 112, 115
Navigation resources, 207
Neighborhoods, assessing, 119
Neighbors
  as informants, 90–92
  suspicious behaviors by, 188–190
New people
  investigating, 201
  self-protection when meeting,
    163–165, 196
News events, keeping current on,
  192
911 calls, 181
Nonverbal communication, 65–69

O

Objects, suspicious, 184, 187–188
Obstacles, in stationary surveillance, 14
Off-grid, going, 113–116
Offsite event security, 125
Online dating sites, 45, 208
Online directories, 44–45, 205–206
Online presence, erasing, 110–113
Online shopping, 152–153, 208
Orders of protection, 209
Outdoor lighting, 131–132

P

Paranoia, preparedness vs., 167
Passwords, 150–152
Patterns, in finding people, 53–54
Peer-to-peer (P2P) file sharing, 146–147, 208
Pepper spray, 165–167
Permission, for electronic surveillance, 25
Personal protection. See Location security; Self-protection
Personal space, 162–163
Personal threat levels, 157
Personal websites, 108, 110, 111
Persons, suspicious, 183
Petty cash theft, investigating, 198–199
Phishing, 147–149, 210
Phone numbers, 32–36. See also Caller ID
Phones
    audio surveillance, 26–27, 29
    blocking texts/calls, 110
    burners, 33–34, 165
    cell phone monitoring, 32
    screening calls, 109
    untraceable, 34
    vishing (voice phishing), 149
Physical evidence, 81–84

Physical surveillance, 1–22
    lying to police officers, 11
    moving, 17–22
    pre-surveillance, 4–5
    risks of, 2–3
    stationary (fixed; stakeouts), 5–16
        (See also Stationary surveillance)
Pickpockets, thwarting, 144
Pinched (definition), 185
Place of employment (POE), 45
Playing dead, 174
Police officers
    lying to, 11
    phony, 121, 168
    unique tax ID and serials numbers of, 122
    verifying identity of, 121–122
Polygraphs, 29, 74–78
Pre-employment interviews, 58
Pre-surveillance, 4–5
Privacy protection. See Identity theft
Private investigation, vii
    author's career in, vii–xi
    qualities needed for, xi–xviii
    real-life scenarios of, 195–202
    resources for, 203–211
    situations using, viii
Private phone numbers, identifying, 34–36
Professional websites, 42–44, 203
Profiling, 53–54
Projective tests, 64, 65
Property ownership, virtual disappearance and, 111
Protecting home and business. See Location security
Protecting others. See Public safety
Protecting private information. See Identity theft
Protecting yourself. See Self-protection
Protesting, as sign of deception, 63–64
P2P (peer-to-peer) file sharing, 146–147, 208
Public profile, reducing. See Virtually disappearing

Public records, 45–49, 208
  court records, 46–47
  criminal records, 47–49
  real property records, 49
  that show assets, 99
Public safety, 179–193, 209–210
  AMBER Alerts, 191–192
  being suspicious of neighbors'
    behavior, 188–190
  and reasons for not getting
    involved, 180
  see something/say something,
    181–182, 184
  suspicious activity or behaviors,
    182–187
  suspicious objects, 184, 186–188
  U.S. Department of Homeland
    Security, 190–191
  working together for, 193

R
Real-life investigation scenarios,
  195–202
Real property records, 49
Registered sex offenders, 210
Reporters Committee, 26
Resources for investigation, 204–212
  offline, for finding people, 49–53
  online, for finding people, 39–49
Restraining orders, 156, 209
Rolling surveillance. See Moving
  surveillance
Run a DMV (definition), 98
Runaway teens, 38, 207

S
Scammers, distinguishing
  telemarketers from, 65
School shootings, 175–177
Search engines, 210
Search engines, finding people
  through, 40
Security cameras, 128–130. See also
  Video surveillance
Security lighting, 130–132, 210
see something/say something,
  181–182, 184
Self-defense moves, 171–172, 198

Self-protection, 156–177
  concealed weapons, 169–170
  constant awareness, 156–158
  disguises, 160–161
  empowering children for, 175–177
  household item weapons, 170, 171
  mace, 166
  pepper spray, 165–167
  personal threat levels, 157
  phony police officers, 168
  restraining orders, 156
  scanning environment, 158
  self-defense moves, 171–172
  during shootings, 173–175
  and social media use, 171
  taking precautions, 158–163
  Tasers, 170
  team scams/schemes, 159
  wearing valuables, 168–169
  when meeting new people,
    163–165
Service workers, as informants, 51,
  85–88
Setting traps, 53
Shootings
  self-protection during, 173–175
  teaching children how to act
    during, 175–177
Shoulder surfing, 142, 144
SILVER Alerts, 191
Sit on (definition), xii
Skip trace (definition), 44
Sliding glass doors, 133
Smart, Elizabeth, 127
SMSishing, 147
Social media
  finding people through, 40–42, 210
  and self-protection, 171
  and virtual disappearance, 109,
    110, 112
Social Security identity theft, 140
Soft targets, 171–173
Spam, 147
Spoofing, 32, 148, 210
Spouse, cheating. See Cheating
  spouses
Spyware, 30–31, 146

Stakeouts. *See* Stationary (fixed) surveillance
Stalkers, 108, 110
Stalking resources, 211
Statements, taking, 87
Stationary (fixed) surveillance
concealment during, 13–14
distance for, 12
by environment, 15–16
lying to police officers, 11
to monitor a vehicle, 14–15
obstacles used in, 14
using drones in, 16–17
Stranger danger tips, 176
Subconscious strategies, used to deceive, 60–65
Surveillance. *See* Electronic surveillance; Physical surveillance
Suspect (definition), 56
Suspicious activity, reporting, 182–187
Suspicious objects, 186–188
Suspicious persons, 183

T

Tail (definition), xii
Target (definition), xiv
Tasers, 170
Team scams/schemes, 123, 159
Telemarketers, distinguishing scammers from, 65
Terrorists, 179–181, 183. *See also* Public safety
Tracfone, 34
TrapCall, 35
Traps, setting, 53
Truth, discerning deception from, 60–65. *See also* Lie detection
Truthfully, guilty person's use of, 63
Twitter, 41

U

Umbrellas, as weapon, 171
Untraceable phones, 34
U.S. Department of Homeland Security (DHS), 190–191

V

Vagueness, 62–63
Valuables
hiding, 127, 135–138
self-protection when wearing, 168–169
Vehicle Identification Number (VIN), 98
Vehicles
leaving valuable objects or information in, 197–198
monitoring, 14–15
for moving surveillance, 17–20
and virtual disappearance, 112
Video surveillance, 27–30
Vidocq, Eugène François, xi
Vidocq Society, xi
VIN (Vehicle Identification Number), 98
Virtual credit cards, 153
Virtually disappearing, 105–116
and bank accounts, 111
breaking laws when, 113, 114
and driver's license, 112
to go off-grid (level 4), 114–116
from harmless but annoying people (level 1), 108–109
and levels of public profile reduction, 106–108
from persistent and worrisome people (level 2), 109–110
from professionals (level 3), 110–113
reasons for, 107
and utilities, 112
Viruses, computer, 200
Vishing (voice phishing), 149

W

Wanted persons resources, 212
Weapons, 133, 134, 169–171, 207
Website locator, 212
What Would Dan Do?, 195–202
Wiretapping, 26
Working together, to protect others, 193
Written communications, detecting lies in, 70